Also by Mark Earlix:

Sedona Millennium Speech – VHS Video

Music of the Spheres Meditation – Audio Cassette

Divine Self Meditation – Audio Cassette

The Flow of Life Exercise – Audio Cassette

i

Creator

Introduction

As I began to write,
a subtle distant voice said:

"As you write, I'll be there.
Find me."

Creator

CREATOR

The Revelation of Healing Your Self and Others

by

Mark Earlix

Creator

5|6³

PUBLISHED BY THE ART OF HEALING, INC.

1928 E. Highland, Suite 104 – Box 144, Phoenix, Arizona 85016
www.theartofhealing.com

Printed in the United States of America

Cover design by Christy A. Moeller, ATG Productions, Phoenix, AZ
Editors: Judith Horwitch and Kathi Diamant

CREATOR/Earlix, Mark D.

ISBN 0-9678058-0-5
First Edition

Dedication

This book is dedicated to God for the 31 years of experience in understanding my gifts.

To my wife for being the best, for being loving, supportive and full of insight.

To Paul and Ruth Blighton, Titus and Karen Hayden, Mark and Mary Anderson of Science of Man (S.O.M.) for showing me the easy way.

To all my staff, especially Suzie Jacobson, Gina Mulroy, Art Duncan, Jill Janisch, Kay Trevarthen and Margaret Barber for their unique support and guidance.

To all my students and drop-ins for being my teacher of experience.

To Judy Horwitch and Kathi Diamant for their skills and abilities to help make this book possible, even with the words that I make up.

To Betty Solomon, Stephanie Felling and Corinne Duhamel for their sleepless efforts of assistant editing.

To the Reverends Joel and Kyra Baehr of Unity Church, Mesa, Arizona and the Reverend Julianne Lewis of the Unity Church, Tempe, Arizona for their continual love and support.

To all those that have lovingly supported me through this project and to those that have patiently waited for this book.

The symbol on the cover and spine of this book represents:
The full functioning of the human-being on all levels of creation.

Creator

TABLE OF CONTENTS

Introduction

Chapter 1: Preparation

Chapter 2: Spiritual Philosophy

Chapter 3: My Story

Chapter 4: Meditation and Directed Meditations

Chapter 5: Intuition, Awareness and Knowing

Introduction

Creator

"It is not, as we see so we believe but, as we believe so we see."

Creator

Introduction by the Author – Mark Earlix

In 1994, Penny, a psychotherapist, asked me to meet with her to discuss the possibility of participating in one of her two-day seminars for the benefit of her clients. The purpose was to introduce my work to help them learn some simple dynamics about spiritual healing.

We arranged to meet at a local coffeehouse. As I sat waiting for her, I found myself thinking how wonderful this opportunity could be for me and how nervous I was to expose my life's work to the world. I did not think that I was prepared; I wasn't sure what to say, nor did I ever dream or expect that what I was able to do in my life could be taught to others. As soon as Penny sat down, we began to map out a plan for our presentation. We decided to take turns speaking. She probed me with questions so I could prepare my portion of the presentation. I was not sure how I could possibly relate my experience with spiritual healing and make it available to each and every person.

My teachers warned me not to go public with what I am capable of doing, lest people come knocking at my door! They instructed that discretion and integrity were of the utmost importance. Discretion is important to let my light shine and the truth be shown. That is the way of the Order. Now I have discerned from my heart those parts of my abilities that can be shared, including the significance of how these abilities can be applied by anyone and, of course, from where they come. As with anything, there are, however, certain aspects of my abilities that cannot be shared.

The following Saturday I was introduced to the 25 attendees. They were a diverse group from varied walks of life. I felt afraid that what I knew inside could not be taught. How could I convey what I felt inside and how I approached a healing experience? How could I teach that which I envisioned prior to a healing? How could they accept what could possibly be happening within the person I work on?

As I started to talk, I found myself transformed. The words seemed as though they were coming from the ether around me and, at the same time, from the depths within me. I watched myself converting from introvert to extrovert. I found myself in a mode of Trust. The words and gestures flowed easily from my mouth, from within me, and I was excited. I remember wondering what I would do if someone were to challenge me. Should I respectfully defend myself or gracefully sit down without further comment? But no one challenged me. They listened intently as the words flowed easily and flawlessly. They realized that I was credible, that what I was expressing was true for each person's life. I watched them listen with their mouths slightly open and eyes wide. For the first time, I saw myself in this extrovert frame of expression. I enjoyed the feeling!

On this particular Saturday, I spoke for a short while and then it was Penny's turn again. When it was my turn to speak again, I took the people through an exercise. It was a closed-eyes exercise my teachers had given me 25 years earlier. Its purpose was to help them to "see" in a more focused way. Halfway through the exercise, a young woman, Melinda, decided to peek, so she opened her eyes. Melinda was able to focus on a non-linear perception, something she wasn't used to.

Introduction

Something had opened within her. Then, the greatest of all my fears came to face me.

First some background information. Twenty-three years prior to this first seminar day I was living in Fort Worth, Texas. I had gone to a bar filled with hundreds of people. While sitting in the front near the door, a large man in leather with a rugged face approached me. He looked at me and simply asked who I really was. I told him my name was Mark Earlix. He began asking me questions about God. I found the answers came easily. He continued with his questions and the words came pouring out of my mouth. As I looked up, I saw that others were gathering around the table. Several others had also started to ask questions, and my answers to those questions also came easily. Others, suffering with health problems, approached and asked for healings. I complied and began to work on many people there.

This went on for quite while (I'd lost track of the time) when a young man edged himself toward the side of the table and asked me to follow him toward the back of the bar where someone needed help. I quickly got up and followed him to a table where four people were seated. They found a chair for me and asked me to sit with them. The fellow across from me rolled up his right sleeve to show me a raised, deep-red, irritated rash. He grimaced and said, " It itches and hurts like hell." He asked if I could help him. Without words, I reached over the table and placed both my hands on the darkest red area. I prayed within myself for a couple of minutes. As I opened my eyes, I saw others gathering and waiting to see what was going to come from my actions. I then put my arms back to my side. The fellow rubbed his arms several times and then began to smile at me as the redness and hurt dissipated.

The young woman sitting next to him watched his reaction, looked at his arm, then at me and immediately became hysterical. Tears streamed from her eyes as she screamed for help and pointed at me. I froze inside; I did not know what to do. The people at the table and those standing around the table watched speechlessly. The screams prompted hundreds of silent eyes to look at me. I wanted to slump down as a numbness and flush overtook me. Instead, I found the strength within me to remain upright. I wanted to get out of there. As I stood to leave, I reached across the table and waved my out-stretched hand quickly over the man's arm, knowing the healing would be taken away as easily as it had been given. Hurriedly, I left. As I pushed and weaved my way through the crowd of watching and wondering eyes, I glanced back and saw the fellow holding his arm as the pain and redness returned. At the same time, the young woman stopped crying. I thought I heard her thinking, or saying, "This is the way it's supposed to be." I never went back.

Fast forward to the Saturday seminar. Now, here I am participating in this seminar and facing a similar dilemma. The woman who peeked had become hysterical and was crying from her experience. But this time I forced myself to stay and began to make excuses for what had happened. I found I didn't want to participate in this seminar anymore, I clamped up in fear, feeling that this wasn't something people were ready to accept.

I have since learned that these experiences were there for me as a stepping stone in my learning process. I experienced these situations because they were there for me to begin to break the mold by the introduction of my teachings. They were there for me to take the old teachings and grow with them in a new, different and meaningful way. These experiences were there for me to learn and understand how to live and how to get out of my enclosed world so that I could go forth into the world I was born to serve.

It is important for me to help people understand that everything is really OK, that we are not unloved or uncared for. We really are not alone, we can find reprieve from the chaos and fear in our lives. That it really is OK to rediscover the trust that was lost at such a very early age. God, the Divinity within, is alive and well within us. God, in His or Her way, is telling us that we have an ability to find Its expression within. We also learn that none of this would be possible without trust. This is when the miracles flow. Not the "woo-woo" or supernatural type of miracles, because we find that miracles are really the way things naturally happen within the activity of life. Great things can happen with us, too, as we realize the potential, the possibility of natural non-linear life.

Each and every one of us has the ability to amend our life's dramas and traumas. We can help make the disease and infirmities dissipate, we can ease discomfort so that some or even all of the effects are gone. The tissue will no longer be inflamed, the bones become straightened, and stresses can melt. The body heats up or we feel the electrical charge or air flowing through us and then we feel clear inside. It is as though we flicked on a switch in a darkened room and the shadows are no longer there. This could happen in the twinkling of an eye, and even before that. This is true healing.

All of this, and so much more, is going to be related to you in **Creator**. You will realize that you too have the ability to work with healing, not only for yourself, but for others as well. This is a self-help/healing book that can help you to actualize understandings and realities that you have only dreamt of, that you thought only a select few could attain. In fact, you can feel better not only in your body, but also about yourself. You will not be led into becoming emotionally or physically ill, as can happen with some self help books. For this book is dictated by a mightier consciousness. This book is about the ability to re-create in Its image. After all, we are here to strive for a sense of perfection. Our purpose here is to find the ability to love oneself, so that Self can express. This will become clearer as you read on and delve more into this unlimited, non-linear world which is much greater than even our imaginations can possibly conjure up.

It was at this first seminar that I realized I could teach this openly and on my own, and I did just that. I have since had the opportunity to teach thousands of people in a one-day "Art of Healing" seminar. Since 1994, after many seminars and lectures, the Art of Healing has developed into a four-day event with advanced modules, healing circles in different cities and developing support and study groups for growth.

This book is a compilation and fine-tuned effort to share many of my experiences from my teachings, seminars, private healing sessions and healing circles. The teachings are a composite of self-guidance and direction, experiences as a healer and healing facilitator. When I refer to living the experience within, I call this an "experientiated" lesson. This book, **Creator**, is the information we already carry within us, but which needs to be remembered. As I come up with the word experientiated, I see the meaning as the "living experience within and in constant action."

Chapter 1

Preparation

Creator

2

*"Judgement of situations, people and
ourselves is a learned way,
not a Being way."*

Creator

I chose to write a self-help, experiential book to teach with the word and with many exercises. These exercises create a quickened change with actual results. I have found no other books on bookstore shelves to match the strength of purpose and results these exercises bring.

Initially, these writings were to be based upon "The Art of Healing," the seminar series I have offered for the past several years. As I began to write, I realized here was an opportunity to share even more of the information from within me, unlimited by the time constraints of a seminar.

Welcome to *Creator*.

Why are you reading this book?

Perhaps you are yearning to fill the gap between the possibilities and realities of your life. Perhaps you have always felt there is more to you than what others see in you. Perhaps you feel there is more to this world than you have been taught to believe. Perhaps you have always felt somehow different, not mainstream, but didn't know why or where to go with this deeply rooted feeling. In all of life's lessons, you sensed something didn't feel true to you or was being left out. Perhaps you are looking for your life's purpose and feel you won't be fulfilled without it.

For all of these reasons and feelings, I have decided to share my life's experiences and the insights and lessons I've learned. Many people have told me that there are those who are yearning for what I have to teach. I present these teachings to you. You may experience either subtle or dramatic shifts in your perception of what is "real"; I call this process of internalizing "alchemical."

Many people are living a life that lacks the expression of love. They may have experienced a lack of love in their developmental years, which has resulted in an inability to be loved and loving as the years go on. Since the beginning of our experiential years, we learned to make excuses for ourselves in thought, conversation and action. We deftly protected ourselves. We taught ourselves (and learned this lesson all too well) to divert ourselves from feeling discomfort. Instead, we get to the "comfortable" place where we have learned to ignore the discomfort. We don't realize it can be changed into real comfort.

The reality is that the very lack that we experience in our life is really our calling to recognize Self, the Divinity Within, and allow it to teach us that which we have dismissed. We are here to experience our downfalls in order to recognize them and to work them out. And working them out may not be as difficult as we have been led to believe. These experiences are actually here for us to become aware of our abilities and tools, and to be able to finally say, "Oh I see you, you're trying to become part of me so I can live you out and act you out in my life. Well, I now choose otherwise."

The existing experience of lack is an opportunity for us to recognize and understand that it is actually external to our psyche. We can choose to review our usual reactions and make adjustments. After that, we have the ability to choose again. All that is required is that we identify our "problematic situations" as "our self-conversations" that started at some time in our lives. We can then understand that we don't have to live the old conversations of the related dramas and traumas any more. As we internalize this in action, the old patterns no longer affect us as dramatically, nor are we participating in them as often.

Metamorphosis

You have opened this book because it is now your time to go through change. Scared? This is true for most people, although they may have longed for changes in order to find meaning to their existence.

Carefully consider what is offered to you as you read this book. It represents an aspect of life for which most of us have strived since childhood. Change is always scary, especially when we've had to mentally and emotionally adapt and change our deepest feelings, when we've had to biologically and physically fight for everything we have in our lives today.

The change you gain from this text comes from within. The purpose is to empower you to recognize your greatness and your striving for perfection. We will be delving into the non-physical, non-linear part of the universe we live within, where there is no separation between time, place or space. I hope to answer many of the questions you have had all your life, those things you have had glimpses of, but have been unable to completely process thus far.

You have been going toward this place all of your life. Now is your time to experience "Self," "God," "Nameless One," or "Divinity." There are many terms and phrases we use to represent God or Self or Universe.

Whichever name you prefer is the one you should go with. Be consistent with it. Find the life within it.

I will be using most of these terms. I will be referring to God in the way that God is in my life. My experiences will be applicable to your own in varying degrees. Each person will pick up things according to the experiences in his or her life. When I'm talking about God, I'm talking about Krishna, Self, Universe, Yahweh, Buddha, Christ, Jesus, Mohammed and all the other great avatars and teachers, I'm talking about the Universal Self. They are all the same living consciousness. This is it. There is nothing good or bad, greater or lesser. We are created in Its image, therefore It is not different than we are. We all have Self within. Self is a part of our lives as a living consciousness.

Self carries the power, force and energy that is made manifest in the immediate and externalized atmosphere, the world within and around us. Self provides us the ability to change the pre-manifestation of thoughts we are thinking at any moment, or whatever we think we believe in. We can choose these things every moment of our lives. I will discuss this in greater detail as we progress.

Much is presented in this book pertaining to Self and externalized and internalized healing, but there is much more, too. ***Creator*** does not attempt to predict what the final result of your experience will be, but it is only the beginning of what is to come.

This book will provide exercises and explanations to help you to experientiate, living in the experience within its many powerful dynamics. It will help you to realize the healing of yourself and others. What a statement! Could this powerfully dynamic consequence be true?

Your first exercise: Focus on yourself

Here is an exercise that may be difficult to practice at first, but will have definite long-term benefits in your life:

> Choose the habit that you dislike most about yourself. Keep going back so you can remember when it started, its initial process, when you first began applying that habit in your life. Then ask yourself, "Why did it start?" Wait until you re-member, which means to bring the members back together. By seeing, hearing, feeling or knowing, the dynamic sense that is most strongly recognized within you will reveal your answer. You can then get an understanding of how this particular habit has affected you in different aspects of your life.
>
> You will find yourself reflecting on the current manifestation in your thinking. When this happens, take that which you have just perceived and literally watch the situation unfold objectively. Review that dynamic remembrance as if it were the first time that you were experiencing it. See if you can find the actual causal moment in your life that led to you to carry the habit with you throughout life, that contributed to who you are and why you are what you are today. If indeed you have found the causal moment, watch what happens in your life with the revelation as it is "to be revealed within." In that moment a healing has actually just taken place. It has been intended to change your life for the rest of your life!

Preparation

This process is so simple and unique, and your transformation has only just begun. The transformation changes your mental perceptions and your emotional reactions to them. Your thinking processes may have produced biological effects within your body that manifest in the destruction of the physical being; the destruction you may have already experienced without knowing, which ultimately leads to the body's death. This exercise builds your ability to watch and perceive sundry ways to go through your individualized metamorphosis.

The idea is to watch the process objectively, without becoming involved in the dramas and traumas you witness. This is not possible unless we try this as a simple exercise and realize that in reality, there is nothing to fear. The truth does not kill or mentally harm us, nor can it make us sick, we do this to ourselves. The truth helps you to see yourself and thereby sets you free.

Open your mind to the big picture concept

Though some of the terms used in *Creator* may seem to carry a religious connotation, I would like you to try to detach yourself from the religious meanings of the words as you read on.

The words I use are defined by their origin of meaning. That is, the earliest meaning of these words from thousands of years ago, before organized religion imposed its idea of what these words should mean. For instance, "Christos" is the Greek ancient word for "light or Sun/Son." "The Nameless One" is an ancient term used before the multitudes of religious people created other names for the presence of God. I ask that you put these "current" meanings aside, at least for now, and concentrate on the philosophical understandings of the teachings which are to follow. I want you to see the overall big-picture concept. **Creator** will help you to rethink your understanding of life. When this happens, I have served my purpose.

In **Creator**, I have incorporated an esoteric concept upon which the philosophy of my seminar, "The Art of Healing," are based. I will guide you through exercises to deepen your understanding within. We must first deal with the healing dynamic within ourselves before we can move on to healing others. After all, how can we possibly help another unless we have chosen to also help ourselves? It is also true that as you put yourself into the position of helping others, you also help to heal yourself.

Going through these dynamic processes is a stimulating experience. As we go through them, we will find we become more objective, without the entrapment of the drama, and will experience a different type of "livingness" within and around us. We will realize that we are affected internally in that we feel more free. We are more centered and more grounded.

We will realize that we are affected externally as we see people acting out of integrity around us. We can also understand what they are acting out, and why. We won't need to stand in judgement and wag a superior finger at their negative behaviors and thoughts because we realize people are acting in the only way they were taught, the only way they learned. For the most part, people are doing the best they know how.

Many times, our lives can get a little off track. I used to work at Motorola as a repair technician. I worked on circuit boards that had tiny chips, 1/8 inch long and

1/32 inch wide. These were the receiver and transceiver mechanisms for signals. If one of them were a little bit off, the whole mechanism would be off. There would be no complete circuit and therefore no signal. We, as people, are basically the same. Just like the little chips, we carry a similar representation within us. Our nervous system carries electrical impulses and waves through us. This signal carries information through and around us into the universe. If a neurological response is off, if our thought processes are off, then we are going to be off, too. Our thoughts will be distorted and our actions will reflect that. At the same time, however, this distortion helps us recognize that something just isn't right.

As we learn about the intuitive process within us, we will find ourselves more in synch with the universe. The intuitive process triggers the dynamic that calls the consciousness of knowing into action. We hear and see through our knowing, and it is all within. It is what ancient mystics referred to as the small still voice within. This voice gets louder as we recognize and acknowledge it. It gets brighter in sight and clearer in hearing. We will cover this more closely as we go on.

You will find that you will be able to see with your ears and hear with your eyes. (This is not a misprint.) Contemplate on this statement and focus in on what it means to you. In hearing this small still voice within, it will help you to go forth and serve. As you heal yourself first, you will find that the immediate world around you is also being healed. This is what is important.

There are many stories of people who have traveled to far-ranging spiritual centers in the world like Nepal, the Himalayas, Bombay, and Sedona. Once they have spent time with "great teachers" and have given up their money and belongings, the teacher, the lama, the guru says, "Go home, it's all within you." That's where it is. Everything is within.

We will tap into that small still voice within that has been waiting all our lives for us to listen to it. It is always in constant flow, never stopping. Always guiding, always directing. It will serve us in our emotional and physiological healing. But in reality, how can we possibly heal anything that God has already made perfect in its image? We are the ones who have abused and distorted the image. We are the co-creators and can freely be destroyed by our dramas and traumas. It is these dramas and traumas that need healing. These are the things we can work on now.

You may experience emotional catharsis or some life changes while working with **Creator.** You may also experience physiological, biological, emotional and spiritual healing changes. You may notice yourself going through changes immediately, or by the time it takes you to complete the exercises presented here, or for the rest of your life. If you apply the information in this book to your life, you will experience healing energy and learn techniques to heal yourself and others that you have not ever experienced before.

If you do not totally understand any particular concept I have presented, put the book down and let the concept sit in your mind for a day or two. Then reread the passages. You may find that you now understand them.

I will introduce various philosophical concepts, definitions and ideas for you to consider. I will include my own story so you can understand where I came from and how I happened to write this book. You will learn a variety of healing and spiritual exercises that will help you to pass through your life in an easier, more simplified way. You will begin to live without the daily conversations that have, in the past, enrolled you in the dramas and traumas and in what you think you know, see, feel and sense as your perception of what life is.

Creator

Chapter 2

Spiritual Philosophy

Creator

18

"Self sees you without judgement.
Self sees the truth,
but you are never condemned.
It does not reprimand or make guilty."

Creator

Part I: Everything Is Energy

There is nothing in this universe that isn't made up of energy. It doesn't matter whether it shows itself as a thought, action or as an object. Science has proven that a thought is a measurable, specific type of energy. Magnetic fields have energy. Electricity is energy. Light is energy. Solid matter is energy. All are made up of different vibrational frequencies, but they are all forms of energy. Measurable energy. Protons, neutrons and electrons all vibrating at different frequencies, all are held together by their individual electrical matrix. This matrix is commonly referred to as electromagnetic energy. In our world, we cannot have the "electro" without the "magnetic" for manifestation. The magnetic part gives the electro both its linear and non-linear form and application in bringing the energies into formation.

There are those of us who are able to feel and see electromagnetic energy in its various forms. We see and feel the electromagnetic force as the union of power, force and energy. As humans, we have an electrical matrix that can be measured scientifically. We produce between 4 to 15 watts of energy. This is what holds our cells together in its definite pattern, form and shape. Without this energy, our cells would fall apart. This is true with anything.

If everything around and within us is energy, our dramas and traumas are also energy. Our mental perceptions are energy. Our conversations are energy. Our disease is energy. Our words are energy. Manifestation of the word is energy. Manifestation of the law of cause and effect is energy. Taking this concept one step further, we can say that everything of an incorrect nature can be easily worked with and replaced with another, more positive and constructive energy. We can call this process healing. This is possible because what we refer to as negative energy is only energy after all. I refer to energy as our *life force*. You have the ability to concentrate your awareness and learn to feel it, see it and know it. We will cover this in more depth in future chapters.

Again, everything of this universe is energy. We can learn to work with this energy to change it to something more constructive and positively meaningful and useful. We can use this energy to help ourselves in our lives and others in theirs. We recognize this energy in many ways. One form of this living-conscious energy is what I call the "small still voice within" or "Self." Self's purpose is to create a transformation and recognition within us that in turn helps to create an act. This act then creates a state of being to do what we think, providing a channel of energy or pathway to manifest what is to be.

Self is energy, but in a different consciousness. It has a consciousness in every aspect of existence to the extent that existence wouldn't be possible without its presence. Self is our source of life. It is the continuum of existence.

Part II: Synchronicity: Law of Cause and Effect

We exist on a never-ending continuum of causal moments, the effects of those causal moments, and the subsequent cause and effect reactions and repercussions.

I use the term "prayer" as defined as everything that emanates from within us and out into the world, every word, every thought, every action. This is energy we send out to the world, the energy that determines our life's existence. We live and interact with others in the world of our reality. I suggest that our every word, thought and action is our living prayer. Prayer is the energy we send into the world, the energy we utilize in our Self for the manifestation of our potential. This is our prayer. This is the manifestation we choose, the unceasing conscious moment. Knowing this, we can develop the awareness that in every moment we can become more conscious.

We generally "pray" three ways: Mentally, vocally, and positively. Our thoughts are our prayer and each one will manifest in some way. Every word, thought and action is our living prayer. Everything we think, say or do provides a causal moment -- that is, it leads to the next moment, the next thought, action, or even an event yet to occur. Everything is on a continuum. I call this the flow of synchronicity, *the law of cause and effect.*

The causal moment is a moment in chaos. Whether in the mind or in action, the moment is undecided in its next course of activity. Amidst the chaos is the potential for a greater pattern, which is dependent upon our frame of reference and the life experiences upon which we draw. Whether it is destructive or constructive, it is still a causal moment. Causal moments are there and available for us to become aware of, as they are a part of us in every moment.

We cannot destroy the memory of the non-linear. We can only rearrange it to a different consciousness. If we become conscious of our causal moments, then we can manipulate and work with them as tools. This becomes easier as we become more conscious of ourselves and less tuned in to the dramas and traumas of living. When we concentrate only on the dramas, we find our thinking processes become cluttered and distressed.

We know that for every cause there is an effect. Consider that every thought is a causal moment. Every time you choose, you have an effect on another causal moment. *Contemplate on this statement, and as you do a new world will be opened to you.* Once you understand this, you will see how things have affected you all your life, how everything you have thought, said and done has made you who you are today.

I want you to understand this: you can affect the causal moments in your life. You have a definite choice of how you want to exist in every aspect of your life. You can rearrange every moment into something constructive, turn it into something conscious and useful. If we could be totally aware of our own thoughts for just one hour or even one day, we would see just what we are really praying for in each moment of our lives.

Cause and effect in action:
Consider the butterfly

Sometime ago I read an analogy by Dr. Pete that I found interesting. It examines the idea that the forces around us are truly connected in a continuum. I'll try to relate it as I remember it:

> *In order for the butterfly to come out of its cocoon, it has to gnaw its way out. During that time, thermodynamic forces are subtly at work at the point where the butterfly is using friction to destroy the cocoon. With friction, there is heat and deterioration. This movement creates other dynamic forces. Then the butterfly spreads its wings in its new external environment and takes flight. As it flies, as subtle and as light as the butterfly's wings are, it moves the air around it. It creates a current in its immediate environment that then ripples outward into the atmosphere. It doesn't stop there, but has a creative effect that flows continuously, nonstop until it affects the entire universe, just as the forces circle outward when a stone is tossed in water.*

For every moment, every thought, there is a continuum that doesn't end. Everything is a part of everything else. A representation of a synchronistic act is the action of a "skipper stone," a stone that skips across the water barely touching the surface. Each time it touches, there is another causal moment and it affects several dimensions as it flows into other ripples. Each ripple is a causal moment that creates subsequent ripples, and so on, into infinity. This phenomenon can certainly be applied to our own minds and actions.

There are effects known and unknown to us, happening all around us, in every moment of our lives through desire, word and action. For instance, simply watching an interaction between two people can have lasting effects. Let's use the example of a fight between your parents. Perhaps they were arguing, and perhaps you were listening and observing the dynamics. How did you feel? Can you remember how your body reacted emotionally? Did the emotions hurt in your stomach or heart area? If this actually happened to you, do you remember what your other reactions were? Did you try to quell the situation between them or did you stand back and wish you could disappear? Did you think, "Uh-oh it's time to be afraid of Mom or Dad?"

Taking these considerations and applying them to yourself, can you see the dynamics at work on you? Do they still apply in some way in your daily interactions in the world? For those for whom these dynamics do apply, how is your stomach and heart today? These effects are the dynamics that have created the patterns and diseases we have chosen to live with all these years. This is one aspect of synchronicity and the ripple effect.

Part III: An Explanation of Self

Seeing and Believing

Many of us think, "I'll believe it when I see it." I ask you to simply ponder an alternative thought: **"It's not necessarily as we see so we believe, but as we believe, so we see."** What we accept, what we believe, will be.

Go beyond the limits of what you know, go beyond the "norm" that you have been taught – that to which you feel stuck. Go beyond this and delve into each and every thing you have learned. Trust what dwells inside, where you will find your true "Self."

Understand that our perceptions are our conversations and our conversations are our perceptions. This dynamic is only a part of what is really happening in the world as we see it. Our thoughts, actions and interactions are within and all around us. Beyond this, there is more, there is the causal moment in our dynamic understandings. We have reasons why we perceive things the way we do. These reasons, in the linear world, come from our self-protectionism, from inside the walls we have built around us in both our inner and outer environment. We must feel safe in our protected environment before we will venture out into the unexpected. We take one safe step at a time. This is our human nature, not yet fully integrated, but learning to become a "human-in-being."

What is Self? God? The Nameless One?

"Self," "God" and "Light," I will use these terms interchangeably as my own points of reference throughout *Creator*.

Self is within. Self is the living consciousness within our bodies. Our bodies are simply shells created to allow Self to express through us. Self has always been there, within us, every moment of our lives. We all have this voice within. But some of us have not yet learned how to commune, become one, with it and make it an empowering tool in our lives. I will teach you the tools you need to be able to hear that small still voice within, a phrase used by mystics of old. That is precisely what it is: a small still voice within. At one point, when I wanted to understand Self more, I asked for a description I could use to help other people understand. This was my answer:

"Self is always there for your guidance and direction. Always there, always waiting. It is always waiting for you to listen. That is why it is here! To guide and direct you back to its Self. Judgment is a human-learned way, not a being-way. Self sees you without judgment. It has no consciousness of judgment. Self sees the truth, but you are never condemned. It does not reprimand nor make guilty. It has no personality as we know personality. We all have the inner voice. All living things have this inner voice, an inner constitution of existence. It has no present, no past, no future. It is in this moment. It speaks to us in the moment, often interpreted as an idea or a thought or a revelation.

Revelation means to be revealed from within, in action. Our understandings, experiences and vision stimulate our sight. That is why it is so important to understand Self, to let it do what it needs to do within us and through us, so we can be free to let it be and express itself. In ancient times, revelation meant to "reveal the reverend, the holy one within." To "revel" is defined as to make merry, to take pleasure and express delight.

> *We reveal and revel as the truth comes forth in celebration. Self strives to help you learn to listen to the "Holy" voice within.*

Self strives to help you learn to listen to the "Holy" voice within. How often and how unnecessarily we sabotage our lives and ourselves by discounting these interventions, thinking that we are just having a fanciful idea which couldn't be real. "No one could be interested in what I do or what I have to say, they wouldn't believe me anyway." How easily we discount our own experience of Self. This is what we are taught to perceive and believe. Where then, is the trust? In reality, it is what you know before another speaks or does something. You know this. You have certainly experienced this.

How does Self perceive Itself?

> *Self has no drama or trauma. Self tells us what is. It is the thing we thought yesterday and see tomorrow, which is today. Self is our guidance and our direction, telling us to stand for what we know*

> *to be true in the deepest recesses of*
> *our hearts. It tells us to trust. It*
> *assumes that we trust and are*
> *trusting. As we well up with*
> *inspiration, Self reminds us that it*
> *is the living force within us.*

Godliness within is a constant "knowingness," that is always available to us. Whatever we want, however we want to be, is OK. Everything is OK. The God I perceive is not a vengeful God. There is no retribution from God. God does not care if you speak in a traditional "holy" manner. Personally, I relate best with people in street language. All modalities serve a purpose. Whether you wash your hands for God, attend church or a synagogue, whatever you do serves as your validity of God. For me, God is beyond religion and religious ritual, although we need ritual to relate to and express that very essence of God. God knows everything is OK. Everything will happen as it is supposed to. Whatever you choose, will be. Trust in that and watch what happens around and within you.

Part IV: Free Choice or Mass Mind: Which Do You Listen To?

Since birth we are given a choice to use our free will to hear the voice of Self. We can listen to the guidance and direction of Self, or we can listen to the world and believe our friends and family, and accept only what we are taught. We can choose to be "accepted" and become part of what I refer to as the "mass mind" belief system, or we can choose Self, where we don't get involved in the dramas and traumas of our lives. We can be free and truly recognize that we are free.

Not all that we learn from the mass mind should be discounted. You still need to how to function in our earthly world. You need to know how to hold a job, how to interact with others and have graceful manners at the dinner table. But other mass mind concepts instruct you on how to respond to people and situations in your life, a more truthful way that is greater than our concept of integrity. As we delve deeper into ourselves, we can see how mass mind integrates into our perceptions.

The negative aspects of mass mind exist to negate and sabotage us. They serve to keep us "in line" and in accordance with how others think. They do not allow us to "get out of the box" or to consider things differently. God is the vehicle for self-expression and self-sustaining life. God is in constant evolution, so that we can become the experience of being "So poised, so perfect, that none but Self can comprehend."

Our dramas and traumas are creations of mass mind. Mass mind teaches us about retribution, guilt and sin, but God doesn't. The God inside me is not a God of retribution or revenge. My God is not saying, "Hmmm, I think I will get even with them today," or " You screwed up," or "Uh-oh, you're going to get knocked down three more notches," or even, "You get one more wish today."

Self has no pain and no disease. Self doesn't deal in guilt and fear. Self helps us to work with pain and disease in momentary situations. Self helps us to truly love ourselves as we give recognition to our Self and the joy of limitless giving and living. How can we truly help another to love and have a greater experience of life unless *we* can truly begin to love? The bottom line is that it is always up to us to choose to listen to the voice of Self. We often say to ourselves, "I will listen, but in a moment. Right now I have to do this or that first."

Self teaches conscious choice

Self teaches that you have a choice in every word, thought and action. Stop for a moment when something is happening to you. You have a choice to say yes or no to your reaction and the perpetuation of it. You have a choice to get involved and react, or you can step back, see what is really happening and decide if you want to react now, or not at all. You might not think you have the time to make a choice regarding your reaction or thought, but you do. You can literally stop at the beginning of a reaction in any situation and decide what you want to happen.

Realize that other people are going through some things in their life, whether momentary or long term. They, too, are clashing and reacting to some aspect of their childhood. This memory pattern deepens as they live their lives. It is their conscious choice. If someone says something to you that would normally hurt you or disrupt your otherwise pleasant day, you can pause for a second, and realize that what they said is meaningless. It is only a temporary, disconcerting situation, and it is theirs to deal with. Now, you can get back to your lovely day and on with your life. It's that simple. It's your choice.

Once you start to make these conscious choices, you will find they get easier each time you make them. We can unlearn the way we were taught to think. As we practice this, we can become more conscious in difficult moments. The very dynamic of being conscious becomes part of your life. It becomes intertwined with your life, and you will no longer need to practice it. It takes over for you. Times of destruction and negation will become fewer and further in between. You will begin to practice saying to yourself, "Wait, I don't have to react to this...." The conversations and dilemmas may feel a bit odd at first, but, over time, it will become effortless.

Consciously apply this understanding for one or two days, then for one or two weeks. As you allow yourself to develop, you will find that you no longer have to consciously apply your concentration to it. It will become a natural part of your everyday life. You will find that you have let go of many of your old reactive patterns. Without really working hard at it, you'll have more choices, free will and power in your life.

Unconscious reaction will not be a part of your "norm" anymore. You will no longer react to the world's destructive activities. Your body will become healthier. Your body will respond to your greater choice of health. This act reverberates in the whole body, mind, and spirit because in reality, there is no separation between the body, mind and spirit. We are an organism, which influences and is influenced.

There is no such thing as time and space in the mind of God. There is no right or wrong, there is no good or bad. These are the perceptions and conversations of mass mind. In the mind of God, whatever we want is what we get. Whatever we accept is what we have. There is nothing more than that.

We are living examples of what we have accepted into our lives. We have choice, and we have free will. This ability to choose is the carrier of our living prayer. Many times we say, "Oh no, I've wanted to get out of this neighborhood and I'm still here." But you are stuck. You haven't learned to reject the patterns you were taught. You haven't realized that your patterns are the patterns and conversations you have taught, and are still teaching and living and reinforcing to others, and in which you still believe. You are still living in conversations left over from childhood. Go into the emotions and ask yourself, "How does it feel?"

For example, a woman might think to herself, "My father was a drinker, and so has every boyfriend I've ever had. Now look, my husband is just the same and he is abusive, too." She has allowed abuse into her life because it has always been a normal part of her thinking and her life. And her children will also carry that learned "genetic code," because she accepts this norm as what life is about.

If you only accept what you have been taught, you think you won't be loved. Or rather, what you think love is. Here's another self-conversation: "My father was a mouse and my mother an overpowering nag. Now look at the woman I married. I married my mother and I'm now my father." How does it feel? Or: "My dad abused me and so has every boyfriend and every acquaintance I have ever had." How does it feel?

As your life goes on have you found that you have a tendency to act belligerently with others? Did your mom or dad think you were incapable of expressing yourself? Do you now have any throat, thyroid, lower intestinal or lung problems? Maybe you weren't able to express yourself before and now you're fighting back to show the world how worthy you are. Maybe you are fighting back because that's the way you prove yourself to the world around you.

The conversations we hold with ourselves, these perceptions conjured up in our minds, are within the grasp of the mass mind. We give these conversations and our reaction to them a place in our daily lives.

You are now becoming aware that Self is alive and well. You are learning how to reach Self and see all the possibilities once this happens. All you have to do is function with it on a conscious level. This awareness will lead to life changing experiences. You now have the opportunity to no longer be stifled by life. We often don't realize that we are stifled because that is how we've been taught, to be stifled. This is totally unnecessary. It is only the "conversation" of mass mind that we have learned so well.

Creator

Chapter 3

My Story

Creator

"It is not, as we see do we believe,
but as we believe, so we see."

Creator

I.   Life-Changing Experiences
On My Life's Journey

It was 1970. Back from Vietnam, I was deeply wounded. My physical faculties, emotional capacities and mental abilities weren't functioning properly. I was down and out, truly in dire straits.

I drifted, traveling around the country, taking jobs that I couldn't hold longer than a week, sometimes not even for a day. My parents had just about given up on me; they didn't know what to do or say to help me. In those days there was no term for Post Traumatic Stress Disorder, much less any therapy to alleviate the symptoms. Veterans coming back from Vietnam just got a few days "R and R" (rest and recuperation) in Japan before being sent home, if they were lucky. I wasn't.

Over the next two years, I was usually drunk or in a violent state. I couldn't stay in a relationship for more than a few days. I didn't care if I got hurt or hurt others. For a while I was homeless, living on the streets. Finally, I wound up in Arizona, at the end of my rope. I decided to end my life.

On the day I decided to commit suicide, I looked around me and focused on the pile of clothes on the floor. My dirty laundry. This one thing in my life caught my attention. I knew that my parents would have to come here to get my body. They would come in and see me lying amidst my dirty laundry. It would be even worse for them. I decided I would first go to the Laundromat and wash my clothes, and then I would come back and kill myself.

With tunnel vision, I could only focus on my dirty laundry, quickly jamming it into my duffel bag. I left the little bungalow I lived in, and began walking to the Laundromat two blocks away. As I got to the sidewalk, I heard a car horn honking incessantly. At first it seemed far away, but as I switched my focus, I realized the car was right next to me. It was breaking into my "tunnel vision" quest to do my laundry. I was angry. I didn't want my focus to be changed. I turned around and saw two women in car. I yelled at them to leave me alone. The honking continued. The women yelled to me, "We'll give you a ride!" I ignored them and kept on walking. They persisted until I finally got into the car. I told them to take me to the Laundromat.

The women introduced themselves as Patricia and Diane. As Patricia drove, she began telling me my life history. She told me things she could never have known. We passed the Laundromat. I said, "Hey! Let me out."

"No," they answered. "We're going to get something to eat and we want you to come with us," and kept on driving. As she drove, Patricia continued to relate the details of my life with 100% accuracy, while Diane sat there smiling the whole time.

"Who are you?" I asked. "How do you know these things about me?" I was amazed and pretty confused.

We pulled into a Mexican restaurant. At that time, I hated Mexican food, but they insisted I come inside and get something to eat. "The food is great!" they promised. Finally, I followed them in and had the best meal I'd ever eaten in my life—chimichangas! I never knew food could taste so fantastic.

My Story

During the meal, Patricia and Diane told me more truths about my life. I couldn't explain how they could possibly know all the details. After we ate, they took me to the Laundromat and dropped me off. I asked them how I could find them again. They told me their address and said goodbye. I didn't have a chance to write it down before they drove away. I yelled after them, "Wait! I have no memory! I can't remember that!" But they were gone, and I didn't know how I would ever find them.

At 7:00 that same night, I was knocking on their door. Somehow, I had found them. Shortly after that, I moved in with them. They gave me a place to live and found me a job. This was the first job I was able to keep for more than several days. The job lasted six months. I was happier than I had ever been in my life. Or at least since before I'd gone to Vietnam. One day they informed me they were moving to San Francisco, California. I went with them.

Soon after we arrived in San Francisco, we went to a three-story gothic-style building. A crowd of regular-looking people milled about in the waiting area. As I sat there with many others, I waited for my turn to go before the esoteric council for my interview. A secretary received calls and then notified people of their turn to go upstairs.

When it was my turn, the secretary walked me up the stairs into a large room. There was a sea of people, all completely silent. There was no noise in the room at all. Then, I noticed an older gentleman with balding white hair, puffing on a pipe. He smiled at me and said, "Welcome! I'm Paul. Have a seat."

I sat next to him. The other people stared at me. Paul asked, "What's your name? What religion are you?" I told him my name and said that I was Jewish.

"Oh!" he said, "We have a lot of Jewish people here. You'll enjoy it. Welcome!"

I didn't know I had made a commitment to be here yet. At that time, I thought I would probably continue to travel all over the country. I didn't know what was going on, if they were going to do something weird to me or if they were going to try to indoctrinate me into some kind of a cult.

The group was called "The Order." The official name was The Holy Order of Mans.

Paul asked, "What are you doing here?" I thought for a moment and answered, "I don't know." As I said this, I found myself delving deep into many layers of thought, through what seemed like secret, barren rooms. And as I shot through the many rooms, I kept repeating, "I don't know." Finally, Paul said, "OK, we believe you." The interview ended.

When it was all over, they accepted me and took me in, although they never actually said, "We accept you." There were no requirements made of me. I didn't have to turn over my worldly goods (not that I had many.) From that day forward, my entire life changed. I knew I was in a unique place. I learned the most incredible aspects of life and what is "real." It was the 1970s, an era of mystique, enchantment and extraordinary phenomenal experiences.

The first day, the council instructed me to go across the street to a little chapel and kneel before the Mary Shrine there. They would pick me up thirty minutes later to show me where I was going to stay. I walked downstairs, crossed the street and knocked on the chapel door. A man in a brown robe opened the door and asked if he could help me. I told him I was sent to the chapel from across the street.

"Fine," he said. "But you don't have to knock. This is a chapel." I walked in. There was no one else there. As he started to leave, I stopped him. "Where is the Mary Shrine?" I asked.

"Over there," he pointed. "Anything else?"

"Yeah," I said. "How do you kneel?"

He looked at me strangely, " Are you serious?"

"Yeah," I replied. He showed me how to kneel. "How come you don't know this?" he asked.

"I'm Jewish," I answered.

"Oh, we have lots of people who are Jewish here," he said and left.

The door made a creaking sound as it closed behind him. If anyone else opened the door it would creak again. Against the wall, I saw a little table with a nice handmade lace doily on it, with a red rose in a beautiful lead crystal vase. On the wall above the table hung a slightly tilted picture of a woman. I straightened out the picture and moved the table around so it was more to my liking. I picked each petal off the rose, and put them in my pocket to hide the evidence of what I'd done. I became very tired, so I figured I now had the perfect opportunity to take a nap. I laid my head down on the table and I found myself in an altogether different place.

The place reminded me of an old English countryside with hedges cut into a maze. I stood there for a moment, and then suddenly found myself standing on a light-brown earthen road, about 10 feet wide. I stood in a low-cut grassy area, next to an old-fashioned, wrought iron park bench like I'd once seen in Chicago. The bench was quite ornate with thin wood slats.

To my left, the road led into a lush, dark green forest. There was an archway leading into it, but I couldn't see inside. To my right, the road led to what looked like an ancient stone monastery with a drawbridge like those you see on old castles with moats. The door, attached by two chains, lowered and became a ramp as it opened. The chains made a noise when the door lowered, but it was not the same resonance you normally hear in our atmosphere. The door was designed to cover a moat, but there was no moat surrounding the edifice.

From out of this building came a procession of monks. There were ten rows of them, four across, wearing long, brown-hooded robes that completely covered their faces and hands. Where their faces should have been, I saw what I can only describe as an opalescent blackness. The monks walked by without noticing me, except for one. He stepped out from his place in the third column of the last row. He took his arms out from his sleeves, pushed his hood back, and I saw he had a beautiful face -- very masculine but ethereal at the same time. He had shiny, black hair. I was struck by how magnificent he looked.

He came over to me and we began a natural conversation about healing. I asked him many, many questions. As he answered every one, I knew inside what he said was true. He also asked me questions, which I answered. Our conversation centered completely on the subject of healing.

The procession of monks then returned, walking back to the monastery. The monk I was speaking to put his hood back on, tucked his arms into his sleeves, and resumed his place in the line. The monks reentered the stone building and the door went up. I felt someone tap me on the shoulder.

I swung my head around. I was back in the little chapel. The person tapping me on the shoulder began to speak. "I'm sorry I'm late," he said, "I'm here to get you something to eat and to show you where you will be sleeping."

"OK," I replied, and we left the chapel. Once outside, I noticed that the daylight was gone. I looked at my watch. I had been in the chapel for 5-1/2 hours! At that moment, I regarded what happened in the chapel as the greatest, most fantastic dream I had ever experienced in my life. I felt fantastic.

The next morning, I was waiting outside for a ride to the new job that had been arranged for me. I would be working at a bookstore called the Rainbow Bridge, building shelves. I had absolutely no knowledge of how to do this, but it was to be my job for next few weeks while I was with this new and strange group of people.

At 7:00 a.m., there was very little traffic on Steiner Street in San Francisco. A block away, I noticed a street bum walking very purposefully, making his way toward me. I watched him get closer and closer, with an increasing sense of dread. I thought, "This guy is either going to spit on me, shoot me, knife me or do something really vile to me." I stood in a defensive position ready for whatever he was going to do. He was a short man, with greasy hair, tattered clothing and a very unkempt appearance. I began to relax, thinking I didn't have too much to worry about from him. He approached until he stood directly in front of me, and said, "Put your hands on my head."

"What?" I said.

"Put your hands on my head," he repeated while staring right into my eyes.

No one was nearby or watching me, so I put my hands on his head. I felt the dirt and then I felt a strange sensation coming from my hands, or from him, or from both of us. Whatever it was, I'd never felt anything like it before. The sensation lasted for five to seven seconds and went away. The bum said, "Take your hands down."

I took my arms down and was totally speechless. He continued staring into my eyes and said, "Thanks for taking my headache away." He walked away and I never saw him again. This strange occurrence was soon to become a routine event.

I went to the bookstore and started working. At lunchtime, I noticed a very tall man who also worked there. He came up to me and said, "I've got a horrible headache." I didn't know why he would tell me this, and I said, "So?" He looked right down at me and said. "I've got a headache." I suddenly remembered my dream in the chapel the night before and, of course, my experience that morning with the street bum. So I said, "Can I try something really strange with you?"

"Sure," he replied. I reached up and put my hands on his head. I felt the same sensation as I had before, but this time it only lasted about two seconds. The feeling dissipated and I took my hands down. The man looked at me in a funny way and said," How in the hell did you do that?"

"I don't know," I said.

Ever since that day in 1971, I have been working to develop this ability within me. I have learned that this ability is there for everyone. Beginning on that day, I began practicing my techniques on people. I would work to heal people every chance I got. I knew that it was a strange gift that I couldn't go public with. For the next fifteen years, I focused exclusively on the needs of street people, the homeless, gang members, addicts and alcoholics, anyone I thought I could help.

Three months after I joined the Order, I was directed to Fort Worth, Texas. Once there, I continued working with healing. I went into healing mode every chance I found, with every person I met. Even if there wasn't anything wrong with them, I still threw my hands on top of their head. I had a job at a Bonanza restaurant. The large staff of employees knew I worked with healing. They would come around and watch me work with healing, even during the busiest times.

From the first day I consciously started working on healing others, I began to take on their problems. I would come down with sore throat or some other illness. Once I even got a black eye! I had sore muscles, headaches, migraines, and some kind of awful lung inflammation.

Everyday when I came home and walked through the front door, my teacher would ask, "What the hell happened to you?" "I don't know," I'd answer, "but it was a lot of fun!" I'd tell him all my stories. I thought it was all so cool. He would then put his hands on my head and get rid of my symptoms. I would be fine, ready to go back to work the next day.

But after a time, my body became weaker and so low on energy that my health started to break down and I would get sick for longer periods of time. My life force was depleted from taking on other's symptoms and illnesses. One day, I decided to stop trying to heal anyone anymore. I was tired of feeling sick, of being tired, of taking on all the aches and pains of those I healed. I decided I was going to quit this healing thing. Forever.

I went to work that day feeling really good, knowing I would never work with healing again, even though it was fun when I did. Up until that day, I went to work and put my hands on people for practice, to prove to myself that I could heal. Now I was done with all of that.

Sitting on the bus on the way to work, I thought, "I'm never going to work with healing again." I told God, "Take this gift, I don't want it!"

As soon as I got to work, an older woman followed by an entourage of co-workers who wanted to watch me work on her came up and said, "I've got this migraine." Still other employees heard her and began gathering around me. I got caught up in the mass mind thought: "Whoa, he's healing!" and the excitement of the others gathering to watch me work. It felt like a party. So, I told the woman to sit down. I took off my coat and had put my hands on her head when I remembered, "Oh my God! I'm going to get a migraine!"

At that moment a new thought came into my mind: "If this healing thing began happening to me without my having any real knowledge of what was going on or having any experience with it, then maybe it wasn't me doing this in the first place." If this was true, I could go back to the first time I put my hands on that bum's head in San Francisco. I didn't get a headache when I worked on him.

I went ahead and put my hands on the woman's head, and at the same time, I said, "God, I don't want this headache, this migraine. I don't want it, you take it God, you take it. If you get a really big migraine, God, that means I don't have it." My logic was that if God had the migraine, then I wouldn't get one.

I felt something happen, a flow traveled through me and dissipated. This sensation was one of my indicators that everything was done. I put my hands down. The woman looked at me and said, "Thanks! It's gone!" I then realized I didn't have a migraine, either.

Since that day I have not taken on other's illnesses because I realized it was not me doing the healing. All the symptoms I had felt for the previous three months were there for my growth. Those experiences were designed to prove to me the reality of my healing ability. Nothing else. I realized I do not have to absorb any illnesses, ailments or anything else from another person.

In 1994, even though more and more people were asking me to teach them how to heal, I still felt I couldn't go public with my abilities. Suddenly it seemed floods of people were asking me to teach them. A psychotherapist I knew approached me and asked if I would attend one of her seminars. She wanted me to participate by explaining what I do, and to attempt to teach it. I explained that I didn't know how to teach. She offered to meet me at a coffee shop so we could talk it over.

Our meeting brought out my ability to write the information down so that I could convey it to others. The first draft was difficult and a little rough around the edges. Initially we came up with a half-day program of activities. But once the seminar started, people wanted more and more information until the program filled a full day's schedule. That was the moment I realized I can teach what I do. And so I have.

The light, which I first became conscious of in 1971, is my gift and my goal. During my initiation process of understanding my role in this world, there was an actual physical and spiritual implosion of light within me. It was a purposeful part of my initiation. I didn't know then that this was to become my gift, my goal and my tool, but now I realize that the light is my life. I work with it to teach and to tune into the world beyond myself.

This light is the source. It has a consciousness. It has intelligence. It knows what to do either with or without our involvement. It uses us. We are its vehicle to reach others, as well as our own selves. I use this light to help heal others. More importantly, I have learned that anyone can use this light. I use it better today only because I have practiced with it. You can choose to practice, too. If you do, you'll find you can do other things as well.

II. Experience of Hearing Self

The first time I ever heard Self was on a Sunday afternoon at a social get-together in 1971. It was a few weeks after I had joined the Order. Incidentally, although I was never actually told that I had been accepted, I have been with the Order ever since I met them, and I'm still with them.

At this Sunday social, there were about six or seven of us standing around talking. I noticed one particular woman standing off to the side. She didn't join in the conversations. She wasn't introduced to me, although I was introduced to everyone else. I listened, waiting for someone to mention her name. (I don't know why I didn't just go up to her and ask her name.) Anyway, I was very curious about her. I wondered what her name was, and I was bothered that I didn't know. Later that day, lying down in my own room, I couldn't get her image out of my head. I thought about her until I dozed off to sleep. Just then, all around me and within me came a booming voice, permeating my whole being, startling me.

It said, "Carol, her name is Carol."

I jumped up, eyes wide, looking for the person in my room. No one was there. I could not figure out where the voice came from. Then I realized it came from within me. No one could hear what I had been thinking; I hadn't mentioned my curiosity about the woman to anyone. I was amazed, and felt a wave of satisfaction wash over me. From somewhere deep within me I was given the answer to my question.

A few days later, I saw one of the fellows who had been at the Sunday gathering and asked him, "By the way, who was that woman who was standing off to the

side? The one no one really talked to?" He replied, "Oh
you must be talking about Carol...."

Over the next several weeks, things started
clicking. I began to realize I actually could hear Self, the
Self I had been learning all about for the past several
weeks. I began to understand what Self is, where Self is,
and how to fit Self into my life. All this began to click into
place, little pieces at a time.

III. 2000

We all have many choices and paths in life. The Order, as it once was, is no more. Part of the Order took on the original name, the Science of Man, and this is the group to which I belong. Everyone in the Order is fully integrated into society and the world. There are no Order houses or communes. I live a normal, everyday life. I don't consider myself a Master Healer yet. But I am growing and will continue to expand my abilities for the rest of my life.

I want to emphasize this point: During the many years I've spent developing my skills, I've come to realize that anyone can do this. Through my teaching, I found that people not only gained insight to the actual act of healing, but were finding other subtle changes taking place in their lives as well. They felt more centered, less troubled, and more complete. They were growing on a spiritual level they hadn't anticipated. An unspoken void in their lives was being filled.

Today, I am an uncomplicated person who enjoys living a simple life. That's my style and it works for me. And yet I know what I am doing now is only the beginning of what is still to come. The same is possible for each of you. People who read this book can have the ability to do even more than I can. It will happen naturally even without your belief that you will be able to heal others. Prepare to be amazed.

Creator

Chapter 4

Meditation and Directed Meditations

Creator

"Enjoy the silence. Revel in what you experience. In the silence is stillness. In the stillness is love.

We refer to ourselves seeking the greater spirituality only because we see ourselves external of It. Yet, if we were internalized, we would not be seeking it from outside of ourselves."

Creator

Part I: Meditation: Where It All Began.

Meditation has been practiced since the days of the cave man/cave woman. Hunters would sit in the forest for hours, melding with their surroundings in order to become one with it, in synch with it, so as not to disturb the environment and scare away their prey. It took a meditative concentrated focus to achieve this. Since that time, thousands of different techniques have been developed. The style I work with operates in a "deeper," rather than a "New Age" sense. With this style you will find it won't be necessary to avoid the reality of Truth speaking out to you. You will have clarity in what's truly real. This is an esoteric approach in my definition of esoteric as "inner teaching."

"New Age," in my understanding, started with the new thought movement that appeared in the early 1800's. This movement taught the inner teachings. At that time in history, much of the world was unable to handle these concepts and so it was watered down to a more palatable level for society during the early 1900's. It was diluted until it reached the point that the concepts became more acceptable to the public. As people spiritually awakened, they began to delve deeper into other aspects of inner teaching.

I'm helping people go back to the Source, instead of being reliant upon someone else's source, or following the path they believe is the only way to the Source. Your way is the best way, and you can get right to Source from within. That Source is Self.

In meditation we can see a piece of ourselves. Our past, present and future has helped us to be who we are, what we are, and why we are today. You can actually see each aspect of your personality in the past, or what we call the past. Your personality exists in what you are portraying in this moment. It is in your constitution and in the living consciousness of every single tissue, cell, bone and muscle. It is alive. It is always there, and has been throughout eons of time.

Every moment in which you are functioning is related to another time and another place. In a meditative state, you can sit down, close your eyes and ask to see a piece of your past. It may come in a flash, but it will speak volumes, depending on how much you trust your receptivity and perceptivity. You will see some part of what you are doing in the present. We all have the ability to access this information. You must remember that there is nothing in this universe that you experience unless you are ready to see it. The purpose is not necessarily to dwell on any past life experience, but to gain understanding of synchronicity and how it applies to who you are today. You have to know that whatever happened all those years ago was preceded by something else that led to that point. What you are going through now is representational of that time, but so what? You are living in this moment. You are working out the "Now."

There is no drama and trauma in what we receive. We can see ourselves, since the beginnings of time, in the composition of material we are made of. We can see the organizational, even atomic formulation that creates our being. Since time began, we have had millions of experiences.

The New Age teaches reincarnation, not as the mystics of old taught it, but in the newer teachings. I speak of reincarnation in the same sense as the old mystics, in which our past goes all the way back to the beginning of time. These moments of old are still carried within us and we can tap into them when we are in a meditative state. This goes beyond the concept of past-life experience and, in reality, each experience can be reviewed in mere moments. In a short period of time, you can learn and understand a perspective of a whole consciousness. Sometimes it happens in the time it takes to blink an eye.

During meditation you will see things that need to be worked out now, regardless of when they originally occurred in your past. No matter what it is or where it originated, it is showing up in your life today because it needs to be addressed now.

Meditation is not thinking. It is receiving information from a greater source within. The mind is your tool of connection between the "spiritual" and the mental, whereas the brain is the tool of reception of the spiritual, mental and physiological effects of what you receive and how you interpret the information you receive.

Ask a question, get an answer

Meditation has little to do with relaxing or focus or concentration or prayer. The purpose of meditation is, in my understanding, to ask a question and get an answer. It is a path to greater awareness. During meditation, you can ask questions on subjects you always wondered about but never learned, and receive actual answers and explanations. You will get correct answers that can be verified by experts in that field of study.

The living consciousness within us has that ability of understanding and knowing. All we have to do is learn how to tune into that consciousness. We will be doing this in a "directed meditation." I will lead you in a meditation to teach the meditative process to you. Once you get the hang of this, you will find that meditation is absolutely applicable in every aspect of your life, even at work or when you are working with yourself or others in healing.

What meditation brings to our lives

When we meditate, we experience many things subconsciously without getting ourselves in the way. What we experience is in direct relation to what we need in our lives. Meditation breaks through layers of intellect, through misconceptions and pre-understandings.

Each time you meditate will be different and unique. Although you have done a certain exercise before, your experience will change because you are at a different place of understanding. Through your senses, you may experience peace, you may experience the dizziness, which I call clarity, you may have felt nothing (though you experienced something, you weren't aware of it). You will always experience something, either consciously or unconsciously. Self is using this experience as the perfect way to reach you in an unencumbered manner. Some people feel "out of it" when they finish meditating. This is because they are in a different world while meditating and their body is simply readjusting to itself when you come back.

Origins of meditative phrases

I have been taught many different meditative phrases, each of which has been purposefully designed to increase insight. These phrases are truly special. They are alchemical in nature and will help to shift your constitution to a more opened awareness. They change you by means of your intent to use them. These are the same phrases mystics used thousands of years ago. The power behind them keeps them perpetuating throughout your life and history. They are inspirational, which means, "to be inspired from within in action."

The following exercises are designed to teach a developmental method that tunes you into your original spiritual mode of perception. This will affect you emotionally and therefore biologically and physiologically as well.

Part II: Breathing during Meditation

In the East, people are taught to breathe through their nostrils. In other parts of the world people are taught to breathe in and out through the mouth. In the West, according to our geographical location and our environment, we bring the best of both worlds together. We can go through a tremendous spiritual experience when we breathe in through our nostrils, as we did with our first breath at the time of our birth, and breathe out through our mouth, as we express our words. We use our mouth to express the manifestation of life. The sound of creation comes forth from our mouth, not our nostrils. The Word is spoken. Breathing in this manner is referred to by some as "breathing in the breath of God" because it is God who grants us life and it is in this way that God is presented to us.

If you are not used to it, breathing in this manner can be uncomfortable simply because you have forgotten how to do it. With practice, it will become more natural.

Breath of God

In breathing in the breath of God, you are experiencing your life source. This is the spiritual side of us. We develop spiritually through the breath of God. It continually nourishes us. It is non-stop and never ceases. It is our very life's existence. It emanates from us, carrying the genetic code of our very existence. It is a constant reminder that every particle, cell, tissue, vessel, muscle and bone of our living body represents in a spiritual sense who we are, what we are and why we are today.

The earth also breathes

The earth breathes. It is alive. Have you ever noticed between 2:00 and 4:00 in the morning, how very different it is from the rest of the day? Unless there is massive storm activity, those early hours tend to be very still and quiet. This is the time the earth is regenerating itself. The earth is breathing.

Part III: Body Position during Meditation (Don't forget to breathe)

Everyone has a unique experience of meditation. You will learn to sense your own meditative state and discover how you can best communicate to become One with the Godliness within.

If you want relaxation, you can lay down during meditation. I have found that the act of lying down leads to a dream-like experience. It may have validity in providing information, but this position is generally not as effective as a sitting position. There's also a greater tendency to fall asleep when lying down.

If you want concentration, stare at something and wait until something happens.

When I meditate, I ask for answers to a particular question or situation. To accomplish this, I sit up in a chair or sofa with my feet placed flatly on the ground. Since more physical balance is achieved in this way, the answers to questions are more balanced.

I have also found that many people on the North American continent find it very difficult to receive answers when inhaling and exhaling only from their nostrils.

In order to receive answers to your questions, it is important to inhale deeply through your nostrils and exhale softly and slowly from your mouth. Pay no mind to any momentary discomfort. Practice. Practice. Practice. If you practice this breathing, it will become more comfortable. If you feel constriction in your lungs when you breathe this way, try this: Breathe in very deeply through your nostrils and expand your chest area at the same time. It may ache and feel tight. Now hold it for the count of ten and let it slowly out. Do this again taking a bit of a deeper breath. It will become easier to breathe this way because you are awakening the cilia in your lungs, which will continue to expand through practice and the breathing will become freer and deeper.

How we are seated during meditation is also important. To get answers during your meditation, place your feet flat on the floor and sit with the crown of your head reaching for the heavens. The lotus position, while practical for other types of meditation, is not as effective for our purpose.

The light comes from above and the crown of our head should be closest to this source. At the same time, our feet planted firmly on the ground respond to the gravitational pull of the earth. This completes the optimum circuit and environment to attain answers. You will have the electro coming in and the magnetic source coming up from the earth as they meet in the center. The solar plexus is representative of the solar system. This is the place of balance within us. There is a universe within us waiting to be discovered. It is only when these two forces come together that the implosion of a whole, greater consciousness occurs.

I have personally tried many different sitting positions with my hands in all sorts of various arrangements. Today, I usually sit in a chair with my feet on the ground and my hands positioned so the fingertips are barely touching. Since hands are our terminals for giving and receiving, I can tell when I am in a meditative state when I no longer feel my hands but feel I am grounded and the energy is flowing through my body. Through practice I have found that I no longer feel my body anymore. I let go of my body in relaxation with my feet flat on the ground.

We will not be denied what we need. Get comfortable in whatever position you feel is best for you. Your meditation will not be altered by what you are wearing, whether a watch, necklace, or beeper (unless it goes off.) God doesn't care; "things" don't matter. Nothing really matters. It's our own dramas and traumas that stop the process, that sabotage us. I teach the position mentioned above to help people break into this type of meditation. Once they get the hang of it, they usually find the position that works best for them. When you start off in this recommended position, it acts to set a focused pattern in action. Make sure you are comfortable and sitting fairly straight. Be as relaxed as possible to be ready to receive. Relax and take it easy.

Think of it in terms of taking a road trip by car. We're in the initial starting up period when you adjust your seat so you will be comfortable sitting to travel a long distance. So get comfortable. Enjoy yourself.

Take along paper and pen

Before you begin to meditate, place a pen and paper near you or on your lap. I often have a writing pad balanced on my lap with a pen in my hand. As soon as I start perceiving something I will slightly open my eyes, and jot down notes.

Music or silence?

I learned to meditate in total silence. When I began, neither meditation tapes nor radio music appropriate for meditation existed. Tools are now available to help you in the process. There is nothing wrong with using these tools, as long as the sound helps to stimulate the awareness within so that It can take over. If the music serves its purpose, after a while you will no longer hear it because you are in a meditative state.

If someone tells you that you need to have a mantra in order to meditate, please remember that mantras were originally created to distract you from thinking during meditation, and to focus on a particular aspect in God. Mantras or chants are tools to help us reach a meditative state in that they help turn your mind away from its busy, active state. In my case, I want to get to the source directly. I don't want to be distracted by tools. The bottom line is to use whatever tools are available to give yourself over to the Awareness Within. The Source is within and it is an exact replica of the Higher Source. It is the same source.

Part IV: Breathing Exercise

Read this exercise in its entirety before beginning. Study the text and what you are looking for as a result of focused breathing. Place a pad of paper and a pen or pencil nearby or on your lap. Once you have done the above, you may begin.

Imagine yourself breathing in the breath of God. Breathe it all the way in, through your sinus cavities and throughout your skull. Breathe the breath of God in through your nostrils, all the way in, and begin to feel the tingling aliveness of your nerve endings, of everything within you. Feel the alertness, the excitement in your body. Notice how the bones of your head feel. The light that you are sensing is actually becoming clearer. If you feel it in your skull, you are not really feeling it in your actual bones, but in the layer of tissue on the surface of your bones that have the nerve endings. This is merely the place where you feel the sensations in the cranial cavity. In reality, a sac surrounding the brain is where the sensory feelings are located. The sac that surrounds the tissue is the area of sensory perception that perceives and emanates discomfort.

Keep your eyes closed and continue breathing. Breathe in deeply through your nostrils all the way to the bottom of your lungs, and exhale slowly through your mouth. You will feel a sense of flow begin to happen within you. Your body is emanating energy. It is the life force within you. It is your electrical matrix which keeps all the cells together. Imagine the tingling is caused by the cells coming alive. Smell the energy as it emanates off you. Keep coming back to "sensing" the energy. It almost pulses off your body in waves. It's very subtle. Tune in to this. Register what it feels like.

Find yourself going deeper into yourself. Sense the energy coming off your body. Conscious awareness is being consciously aware of what is going on around you and within you. Sense the pulses of energy coming from you. If you perceive something, slightly open your eyes, or keep them closed if you can, and write the perception on your pad of paper. Keep going deeper within yourself. Continue with the breathing; notice if it has changed. Perhaps you notice the slowness of it and the lack of breathing. It is the breath of God nourishing you.

Our senses provide a different experience of what we initially thought were our perceptions, and we realize that our previous perceptions were misconceptions, both externally and internally. Our judgements have been based on perceptions we were taught. Notice also that a different perception of smell can bring understanding. Smell can bring up an inner memory of something you had forgotten or were unconscious of. If you perceive something like that, write it down. It will bring up a feeling, a knowing, a thought, or a sense. Go within and find out what it is. Write it down.

Now, with your eyes still closed, starting with your feet, slowly scan your body. Use your internal senses. You will discover areas of discomfort or areas that need work. Slowly work your way up, exploring your body in its entirety. Say to it, "Talk to me. Tell me or show me what you want to show me or tell me." Keep going back to your body. If you perceive something, write it down. As you scan your body, repeat, "Talk to me. Tell me or show me what you want to show me or tell me." In your mind, listen to the silence, and pay attention to the pictures, sounds and colors that come forth.

Focus on this scanning process while working your way up your body, looking for information, as you say, "Talk to me. Tell me or show me what you want to show me or tell me." Practice quickening this process by moving your awareness faster. Stop at any spot you feel dysfunction. Keep talking to It to gain insight. You will perceive answers. When you have worked your way all the way up, slowly open your eyes. Slowly open your eyes.

Read what you have written. Does it make sense to you? Does it provide you with a different understanding?

In meditation we can focus on a particular place in our body where we feel discomfort, whether it is temporary or part of a disease process which you feel on a regular basis. We can say to the area of our body which feels the discomfort or pain, "What do you need? What do you want to tell me? What do I need to do?" And it will give us an answer. This is just one way to work with the meditative process. It will literally give us an answer.

Much of what you perceive from this exercise will be absolutely new to you. You are literally breaking into another world. This other consciousness is waiting to provide information to you. It never ever stops guiding and directing. It is continuously full of information. You perceive just a piece of it at a time.

You might not have the experience of smell during the exercise. That's fine. It means you were going through other things that were necessary. If you are able to smell an odor, recognize that it is only energy. A seed has been planted. Your engines have started. In some cases, these engines are being started for the first time in this life. Over the years, they became clogged. Now we are tuning into the Divinity Within which will clean out the cobwebs and the rust. That is what the light does.

At times during meditation, we won't remember anything, the time will seem like a blank. You might think you were asleep, but you weren't. When this happens it is because Self knows when we will be getting in the way so we are taken out of the way. I relate this to when someone has surgery and is given anesthesia so they don't experience the pain of the procedure. When they awaken, the necessary changes have taken place even though they were unaware of it while it was happening. This is the same thing. Self protects us. We are not given anything more than we can handle. We are given a lot, even if we are unaware of all that was given.

Part V: Meditations:
"Divine Self Meditation"
and "The Flow of Life"

Here are two ancient exercises, which have been purposefully developed to teach us to focus within. Originally known as the "Egg Exercise," Divine Self Meditation directs you to become open to communicating to the Divinity Within, the Self, and the Source. You will interact in another world and understand what Self is.

The Flow of Life was designed so one can tune into the flow of energy between the earth below and the sun above. You will recognize your part in the synchronicity of energy's flow.

For best results, listen to my tape "Divine Self" while you are completing these exercises. This way, you will be taken step-by-step through the exercises and can experience a greater adventure.

Divine Self meditation: A guided meditation

I was introduced to this exercise while in the Order. It is an ancient exercise, dating back thousands of years and carried forward since that time. As a guided, directed fixed meditation, you don't have to do anything except listen to the accompanying tape.

To begin, turn down the lights. If you do not have a tape, please ask a partner to begin reading the exercise below:

Put your feet on the ground and your hands on your legs, either up, or down, or clasped, or fingers touching, whatever is comfortable. Just breathe in through your nose very slowly and slowly out of your mouth. Close your eyes. Breathe in and out slowly.

In ancient writings, the egg represents the one who has attained self-realization. The egg has always been the symbol of truth. This exercise is designed to bring you to a conscious atonement, or at-one-ment, at one with health, clarity of mind, deep visualization, peace, and awareness to see the light within. To the initial experience of contact with Self or the conscious divinity within. To the Nameless One, as mystics of old called It and its embryonic state that composes the universe. To the fluidity that carries the mind of the Nameless One that we dwell within. You will experience an overall sense of well-being and peacefulness within. You may also see things, and experience changes in your mental perceptions within two weeks of practice. You may notice a slight glow in a darkened room, a light around yourself during or after the exercise while in a darkened room. This is a natural result of practicing this exercise.

This is a true spiritual exercise in a mystical form for a greater effect. You may experience improvement in health and well-being as a result of this exercise. These spiritual exercises are your opportunity to attain self improvement, and should not be taken lightly. The more you practice, the more you will be transformed. It will quicken your mental and spiritual growth and even your reality. Your spiritual senses will not be externalized, rather internalized through heightened awareness of the Divinity within. Conscious application of this exercise for twenty minutes a day will enhance your awareness within of the Divinity within, or what is known as Self or The Nameless One. Use moderation in the practice of this exercise. It should not be done more than twice a day, or for more than five days in one week.

As it is written: Nothing secret will remain hidden. It is through Self that all things will be shown.

Let us begin. Sit in a relaxed position, in a straight-backed chair, feet flat on the ground. Let your arms drop and then your hands. Let's clear your mind now. First breathe in slowly and gently in through your nose and out through your mouth. It is written that God, the Nameless One, breathed through the nostrils of man and woman and gave them life. If this is true, then we are breathing in the breath of God. Breathe in slowly through your nose, and gently out through your mouth. Breathe deeply down to the lower abdomen. With each exhalation, feel all tension leaving and your body becoming more relaxed with each breath. You will find yourself becoming lighter and more euphoric. You might feel the sensation of a slight electrical charge silently flowing through the terminals of your fingers and your toes and right below the surface of your scalp. The feelings are the fluid of the spirit moving through you. There is no need to consciously let it flow out of you. Feel it well up within you. Continue with a very slow breathing pattern throughout the exercise.

Imagine a slow series of waves moving through your head. Become comfortable with it, let it flow freely. This will allow your cellular consciousness to shift without interference. Now be aware of the waves as they slowly move downward into your throat and through your spine. Downward through your chest. Down through your arms and hands from your chest to your lower abdomen. Let it sit there and feel the waves from your lower abdomen to your ligaments and muscles that bind your hips as it surges through your legs and down to your feet. Allowing the fluid of the spirit to well up from within, imagine these waves going through your entire body, from head to toe. Your whole body is becoming more relaxed and lighter and clearer. Stay conscious of your breathing. Feel the clarity and lightness in your entire body. Visualize yourself within an oval-shaped egg filled with clean, clear effervescent, bubbly light. Subtle light is emanating from around you. This light creates a shell around you, a shell composed entirely of light.

You are actually seeing your true self with light emanating forth as you watch this experience. Now imagine yourself standing or sitting or even suspended there. The experience will be unique unto yourself. Continue to breathe slowly in through your nostrils the breath of God, the breath of the Nameless One, of the Universe and slowly out through your mouth through which the Word comes forth. Slowly become one with the light of the shell around you. Watch the light from within pulsate outwards. Focus on the pulsation. Watch particles of light illuminate in the way that a match flares into brightness. The tiny particles of light, in that moment, create a series of waves. You become enlightened within the form you carry. Watch your arms reach up into it. Feel the sensations of the light carry through your being of clear form. Feel it flowing freely. Now, step out. Move out of the shell. Be aware of the light from your form. Feel the emanations from within you coming through you. Feel the joy of its expression around you. Very slowly move in and out of the shell. This will help you adapt to it and it to you; the shell, too, has a living consciousness. Experience the freedom and joy and health of what you truly are, what you see inside and outside the shell. Experience the peace, quietude, intelligence, wisdom and consciousness of the subtle light and its life that gives you life. Now go back into the shell. Slowly bring this consciousness into your physical being. Remember your experience from within. Feel it, sense it, and let it live still within you. As you do, you bring this consciousness back with you into the atmosphere that emanates around you. Slowly come back. As you do, bring this consciousness with you. Slowly come back. Slowly open up your eyes. Sit still for a few moments.

Take a little time to recoup. Stand up slowly and move around. When you are feeling ready, you may continue to the next exercise.

The Flow of Life

This exercise might be somewhat difficult the first or second time you attempt it. It is not necessary to trouble yourself if you do find a lot of experiential saturation.

As you work this imagery, only go as far as you comfortably can. It is wise not to overdo it. Then, go back to it again later that day, or the next.

The purpose of contemplative imagery is to help you to become more at peace with your Self and to be healthier. It also will help you to become more spiritualized in your focus and experience of the oneness of the God-Self within.

Again, if you do not have the accompanying audio tape of this exercise, ask a partner to read it to you with a steady cadence.

The Flow of Life:

Contemplative imagery exercise

Part 1

Begin to quiet down inside.
Let your eyelids drop and relax.
Breathe slowly and evenly...
In through your nose and out through your mouth.
Slowly and evenly...
Begin to feel the flow of life through out your body...
As it begins to flow...
You begin to get in touch with it... the flow.

From your heart, know that
You can feel a sense of love...
The Love that God might possibly have for you.
We know that this love is hidden within the deepest
Recesses of our heart...

Let the love slowly come out from your heart into the
Surrounding areas in your chest,
And it begins to spread outward.

Know that in our natural spiritual state, we too are
Composed of effervescent light filled with Its joy of
Being,
Naturally fulfilled within the love of God,
And that initially we came forth from that love.

This life, comes from within the mind of God,
Of pure life and consciousness, from the mind of God

Meditation

The clear feeling, the euphoric feeling that we are
Sensing, is a result of opening your heart and mind to
It,
Trusting it, allowing it,
And allowing your true Self to
Be fulfilled with the love of God within.
And it filling and being fulfilled... Within You.
Get comfortable with your Self, and let your Self
Become a friend to you, watch yourself becoming more
Quiet.
Allow It to love you.
Let the flow of God's love express its Self in you...
Naturally and without your interference.
Breathing slowly and gently
That this flow might move freely in you.
In Its expression of love in you.

Allow all the thoughts... of other things,
Other times and other places to just flow away
And watch them dissipate into nothingness,
That you may begin to focus... on your true Self.

The feeling and the senses within it...
Sense the fear of doing this exercise, of letting go of
Everything else.
Watch the fear melt.

Allow your body to relax, feeling your muscles and feet
And arms and hands as they keep dropping,
Let them drop even more so.

As you watch the tensions and worries of the day...
Of Life...
Watching them flow slowly away...from your
Awarenesses and your body...
Feeling the flow of life flow through you as the trust of
The fear lessens within you, and the Godliness within
You becomes more manifest.

Part 2

Begin to feel the slight electrical charge as it feels
Prickly
In your hands and in your feet and below your scalp
Focus on your hips
And focus in the pelvic area of bones and muscles and
Small organs within.

Visualize a nerve network almost like roots growing
Through the muscles, the bones of your thighs and
Your legs, as they develop and search for their source
Of life... Just as roots do for water, flowing and
Searching and reaching down into the earth
As a conscious network of veins and capillaries...

Sending the roots down through your body and
Spreading down into the raw fertile earth

As they branch out in search of life...
Through the earth, and growing deeper...
The roots of a mighty tree.
Imagine your roots going down through the many
Layers of the earth.

Meditation

Down through the layers of the soil, through the sand,
The silt, the gravel and the stone...
Reaching deep into the earth towards its core.

Know that the entire earth contains magnetic energies
And that these energies are also naturally a part of
You.
Begin to feel the magnetic energies of your body
As they are also a part of you... to draw upon freely.
Know also, that the consciousness of the earth
Energies are magnetically attracted to you too.
And that your body feels and knows that too.

Feel your roots growing downward,
Moving through the depths of the earth until they
Begin to enter the periphery of a mass...
As though the mass carries a massive presence
Of fire and magnetism.

As your roots just begin to break through the
periphery of the mass,
These roots also begin to connect with this mass of
Energy within the earth
You begin to sense and see... that it is a deep shade of
Blood red and gold energy. And it carries the sound of
soft and powerful rumblings.

Try to perceive this energy mass vibrating eight times
In a second
And as it vibrates, it helps us to keep our own body's
Cycle near a rate of sixteen pulses in a minute.
Watch it and feel it as it feeds your pulse of life.

Creator

This mass vibrates at the same frequency as a
Naturally healthy body.
And as your roots enmesh into the mass of energy and
Become one with the mass,
They automatically attune to the vibrational pattern
Of this mass of energy.

This mass is the earth's blood, the flow that sustains
All life on earth.

Pull this blood-red and gold of the earth up into and
Through your roots and nerves.
Watching the energy as it moves up through this
Network,

Slowly at first,
Begin to feel the sensation of the bottoms of your feet
Wanting to open wider... as though they have vents...
Thirsting for this life.

As you begin to trust it,
Feel it freely flowing more into your feet,
The more your vents open the less fearful it will be.
Imagine yourself wanting more of it

Feel the magnetic blood-red and gold flowing into your
Ankles, up to your legs, up through your thighs and
Into the muscles that bind your hips.

Feel it flowing into your belly, and slowly into your
Solar plexus area, and then permeating into your
Chest cavity,
Flowing slowly... into your heart.

From your heart through your arms and from your
Arms as they fill,
Permeating this life flow into your shoulders and up
Into your throat and then into your spine from top to
The bottom and back up again into your head as the
Mass slowly swirls within you, as it gives you life.

Feel your heart fill with this blood-red and gold energy
Of the earth.

Notice the feelings that this magnetic energy creates
In your body... as it brings you to greater realities and
Sensations,
A different understanding.

Notice the sensations,
You may be feeling a gravitational pull to this source
Of life from the earth.

Allow this earth energy to gently warm the inside of
Your chest and heart as you begin to feel it...
Feel this energy, as it gently and pleasantly warms
Your chest.

As it flows throughout your body and heart, in
warmth.
As you feel your heart pumping in strength of the flow.
Feel the warmth of the flow of the energy moving
Through you.

Part 3

Turn your attention to the top of your head.
Picture a slightly glazed window in the top of your
Head...
And look through the window outward.
Try to decipher what you are seeing as you look
Outward.

Watch as the window's glaze dissipates to clarity.
And that there is no longer the obstruction,

Feel the flow of light,
Its waves and Its particles of energy...
Beginning to flow through you.
Envision this light as effervescent clear glistening
Light,

And in Its wisdom,
It will help you to become more aware of the
Manifestation of the Godliness within you.

Slowly bringing the flow of the clean clear effervescent
Light...
Into the top your head, and slowly down through your
Spine.
Imagining your spine as it is filled with this clear
Healing light

The more you allow it to manifest within you,
And permeate you, exhilarate you,
Notice how differently you feel.

Experience this healing light filling your entire being
As it begins to freely flow throughout your body,
Without resistance.
As its healing light generates into your entire being,
Also watch as it generates outward from your body...
And around you into your energy fields which you
Generate.

Continue to bring this light through the top of your
Head,
Down through your spine.

Notice that your heart is also full of light
Sense how it feels as it fills and nourishes your heart.
Let the sensations expand,

Allow it to completely fill your chest cavity,
Saturating you... with clear effervescent light.

Part 4

Once again, from your feet, pull in the deep blood-red
And gold earth energy and its magnetism...
Up through your feet,
Up through your legs and up into your pelvic area,

Moving towards the stomach and into the chest...
Bringing it more into your heart and saturating it.

Try to visualize and imagine the mixing of both these
Energies,

Of the clean clear, effervescent healing light
And the deep blood-red and gold earth energy...
Both swirling within the heart, blending together.
As the swirling mixture within your chest
Fills your heart.

Watch as the valves of your heart open fully,
Distributing the mixture of magnetism and light.

As it is carried into the vessels, the veins and the
Capillaries... into the cells of your body.
Throughout the wholeness of your body.

Sending this blend of energy down through your arms
And legs.
As it flows to the very tips of your fingers and toes.
And you feel your fingers and toes and scalp with a
Slight electrical sensation.

Part 5

Now, silently and slowly, bring your hands together
Barely touching...
And gently rub your hands... barely touching palm to
Palm.

As you keep your hands still, continue to visualize the
Pulling through your feet the earth's magnetism
With the electrically charged energy of light flowing
Thru you ...
As they mix together,

Breathing deeply and slowly,
In through your nose, down to the lowest part of your
Belly, slowly, out through your mouth.

Meditation

Slightly and slowly pull your hands apart... only three
To five inches at the most,
Feeling the energy surging ... filling your hands
And your wrists.
Feel the small mass of energy between your hands...
At the periphery of it, as you slightly move your
Hands... Slightly closer and slightly farther apart –
It is not necessary to overdo it.

Feel the magnetic pull of energies between your
Hands,
As you bring your hands slightly closer,
The attraction.

And feeling the repulsion of the pulse at the further
Distance
As you slightly separate them.

Very gently, feel this energy on the surface of your
Hands.
Feel how it in some way, it might be affecting you.
Get to know it a little.
Try to understand it.
This is the life force that you carry fully embodied
Within.

This energy is your gift, your very life.
When in times of sickness and distress...
It slightly deteriorates and needs to be resupplied.

When it is totally depleted through the lack of
Creativity and oxygenation and blood flow in the body
And brain, we cease to exist.
This energy is in every cell, between every cell.

It also forms your electrical matrix within and around
Your body
And extends outward into and thru the universe.

It is the energy field that is able to carry the
Information of your life into the aura,
The information of the morphic field within and
Around you.

Take a moment to perceive it.

Now, gently place your hands on your lap.
Focus again on pulling up the deep red and gold
Energies of the earth.
From that mass of energy deep within the earth,
Into your body and again filling your heart
Focus again on the luminous electrically charged light
Flowing into your head…
And also flowing into your heart.
As you watch the swirling motion inside your heart,
Warming, opening and melting the layers of veils that
Have been created to hide the love of God within,

Of what you thought and have been taught was
Protecting your Self from the world of hurt.

Feel the love of the radiant sun,
In all Its magnificence,
And Its manifestation of the Godliness,
The divinity within, bringing life into your heart,

Feel it fill your heart,
And your body,

And the many fields that emanate forth from you
Around you. Try to imagine how it might feel to
You...living within the mind of God
The unlimited magnitude of the information that
Might be offered to you.

Part 6

Experience the gentleness, the joy, the reality of this
World...
Knowing now that we have a choice of which world we
Choose to live within.
Take a moment to enjoy this.
Try to feel it with all your heart. Open your heart.
This is your living God,
Unconditionally loving you and giving to you,

In the way that you always have wanted to feel... and
To know Its love

Feel Its love within you,
Expressing Its love to you.
And when you get ready to come back to the room,
Slowly open your eyes...
And bring this love back with you...
Slowly open your eyes.
And bring Its love back with you...

Begin to come back now.
When you are ready, slowly come back to this room
And slowly open your eyes.

Part VI: Meditating for an Answer

In what form do answers appear?

Meditative answers come in many forms. Answers may come in words, in sounds, in pictures, in writing. They will come in whatever form works best to suit your individual needs. Your answers will find the best way to reach you, depending on your life's experiences and needs.

I met a little girl, nine years old, who was able to see things above a person's head. She would see a fortune cookie strip which, in a few words, would state everything about the other person's world. Her mother was open to what this represented. She did not taint the girl's ability and so it was able to develop. The girl came to me and together we were able to help her develop her knowing, without any sabotage from the outer world. Her understanding excels because she is being taught that this is a natural part of our existence and is not to be dismissed. This is her tool. Each of us has tools to improve our ability to work with ourselves and others. No one lacks this ability, but if you are aware of it then you are able to experience and develop this natural part of your being. Our gifts are made obvious and alive through the meditative process.

How to begin a meditation session

I begin my meditation with a prayer about what I want to know, or I give glory to something or someone. I give thanks for the gifts I receive.

If you are sitting in an exam and need to get the answer to a question, you can go right to the source, the author, and tell him/her specifically what it is you need to know. Make it a statement such as, "Hey look, Mr. Author, help me to understand (fill in the blanks). Help me relate to what you've written so I understand." Then as you enter the test, once you have closed your eyes and made this statement, said this initial prayer, you will begin to get various answers.

You are going to notice, if you don't meditate frequently, that parts of your body might start to feel uncomfortable. That's because you are breaking into a new world. You may not go through this yet; you may experience this in a few days. You may feel like you have the "shpilkes," a Yiddish word for feeling jittery.

If you need clarification about something you read in a book, reread the passage a few times, close your eyes and think about it. Then let it go, and wait. Or you can write the question down in the sky of your mind's eye, and when you have it all written out, step back in your mind, or physically, and wait. An answer will come to you. Wait patiently. You won't go without a result or an answer for what you need. The process only works after you have let go of the question or the expectation of an answer. It is the process of waiting without the understanding how you will receive your answer.

One person I worked with was a student who tried this technique during a test. The student provided information that came straight from the author but was not in the text prepared for the test. The teacher, a professor, asked the student where he got the information, and the student replied, "I just knew it." Remember this very important point: whatever is necessary for you, at that moment, is what you will receive from your meditation.

With meditation we take the helm in providing direction and focus of what is within the universe. Each night, there are as many as three to five billion neural interactions within your body, each working to continue the flow of what happened yesterday and the effects are for tomorrow. When we meditate, we achieve some control over these neural events by providing focus and intent. If you have a specific question or statement you want clarified, your answer will happen in the moment, that night, or the next day, but it will be there for you. You just have to ask.

If you find yourself becoming distracted during meditation, concentrate on your breathing to help bring you back to stillness, the place you want to be.

As we work with meditation even a little bit, the dramas and traumas, the chaotic thinking, the little movies of our lives dissipate to almost nothing. They don't have room to exist anymore.

Meditation

When we meditate, we are naturally opening our sight to God and we find ourselves astounded.

If you are to learn something, you will be told or shown what it is---but only if it is your business to know.

Meditation is a tool to teach us. It is a tool for us to tune into in order to gain understanding of myriad subjects...as long as it is our business to know, and as long as our awareness does not interfere with another person's development. If we know something about someone, there will be a consciousness that we are affecting. Often I have asked questions about a person and been told, "It's none of your business." I understood this and did not take it personally. If you need to know something, you will be told or shown what that is.

Part VII: Our Perceptions after Meditation: How you may feel; what you may have learned

When we meditate we experience a lot of things subconsciously without getting in the way. This experience is in direct relation to what we are going through in our life. Meditation breaks through layers of intellect and misconceptions and pre-understandings that we are not used to. Every time you meditate it will be a unique experience. It's just like picking up words of wisdom from a great book. Read it once, you will get something out of it. Read it again, and you will get something else from it. And so on. In meditation, you will receive that which correlates to what and where you are in that moment.

So even if you have done a particular meditation before, you will experience it differently every time because you have a greater understanding. The first time you do a meditative exercise you might come out of it feeling a little foggy or dizzy. In reality, it's clarity. It's just that you are not used to that feeling. As you develop into meditation, these things will dissipate, they will no longer exist and you will gain many insights. The foggy/dizzy feeling is the resistance that your body and mind are expressing in response to meditation, because it is breaking through the resistance to be realized in this world. Your mental, emotional, and biological constitution is expanding. It is really no different than an athlete developing muscles through exercise.

The fact is, you are experiencing something and something is being done. You have to get out of the way completely. You will always experience something either consciously or subconsciously. Some people feel "out of it" when they finish meditating. That is because they are in a different world while meditating and their body is simply readjusting to this world. What you are really feeling is "in it."

How to know if what you are perceiving is true or psychic junk mail

Many years ago, when I first started meditating, I would get all sorts of visuals. Some were normal, some were filled with weird beings and scary images. I asked my teacher what was going on. How would I know if these images were something of meaning for my life?

He gave me a technique to use during my meditation that I am now passing on to you. This works great. Whenever you perceive anything in meditation, no matter how uplifting or inspirational it may seem, or whether it is gross or disgusting, do the following: Whenever you perceive something, and before you get carried away into believing it, no matter how magnificent it seems, tell this perception to "stand in the light" and watch it. See what it does. See what it becomes. Why? Because no darkness, no falseness, no shadow can stand in the light. It will dissipate. Because no matter how grandiose it is, no matter how revelatory it seems, no matter how valid it may feel, if it is not true, it will fade. On the other hand, if something shows itself to be true, it will persist and take on an even greater form.

After you have used this technique for a while, you will grow to understand what is valid and what is not.

You will have your own indicator which will act as a barometer. Once you have grown accustomed to distinguishing between fact and fancy, you will then begin to immediately assess when something you perceive is valid. You will sense that this is Truth.

Challenge everything in meditation. Ask for more and more elaboration or clarification on that which you receive. It will teach you even more. Keep challenging, keep pushing until you know that everything has been answered in its entirety. You will know when you reach this point. Do not rest until you feel fully satisfied with the response. Use the statement, "Stand in the Light," with the authority from your heart. Don't be wishy-washy about it, say it with direction and focus. Say it to knowing and intent, or don't bother saying it at all.

Part VIII: Conscious Awareness Exercise: Take It One Step Further.

Please read this in its entirety before you begin.

Stand facing a partner. In order to develop your intuitive awareness and meditative skills, we must first discuss conscious awareness. Conscious awareness is the state of being consciously aware of what is going on around you and within you either in the conversation or actions in and around you.

Look your partner in the eyes and keep watching them. You must be able to control and stop yourself and become aware of what is happening within you, with you and around you. I want you to consciously stop yourself in the conversation you are now having when another person is in front of you.

Look deep into his or her eyes. Stop your thinking process that is wrapped up in the conversation. Stop the thought process and go within yourself and see what is really being said and what is really being done within you. Watch the other person think. Try that for just a moment. That is all that is needed, a moment in your life.

Go within yourself. You will see that moment has no specific time or duration. Watch you partner within. Surrender to your Self for this insight. Communicate with it within your mind and as you do, feel the warmth and the flow of it flowing freely through you. Unbeknownst to you, you will then be taken into this process and you'll be able to tune into a new, more real conscious awareness.

With all your heart and soul, feel the love coming forth from within you. Consciously talk to It from inside your head. Express to It within yourself your need to love and listen as It tells you Its need to love you. Realize It as a close friend. Become aware of It. You can almost touch It. This is what awareness is. You are taking it on, you are clothing yourself with It. That's awareness. Let It flow through you. Let It live through you. Let It love you. Feel the love of It. Let It finally express to you Its love for you that you have not felt since birth. Now, come on back.

Part IX: Retrospective Exercise
To Improve Your Focus

What helped me learn to have concentrated focus was this "Retrospective" exercise. This exercise is to be done when you lie down to go to sleep for the night. It will increase your ability to focus. Have your eyes closed or open, it doesn't matter. See yourself in what you are doing at that moment. Then go back through your day, remembering one fairly significant event that happened right before bedtime. Don't get wrapped up in it. Pretend you are watching a movie when you are recalling this event. Perhaps it was a conversation that occurred, or you participated in an action that led to a significant outcome. Now, go to the event that was significant or fairly significant that happened prior to the first one. Something that was upsetting, something you argued about, something you said or thought that was of either a positive or negative nature. Then remember something that happened prior to that, working your way all the way back to when you first awakened for that day.

At first you may not be able to put things in their exact order, but that doesn't really matter. You will find yourself achieving a more precise order as you practice this exercise day after day. It will take care of itself. This is a fantastic exercise. Your memory will be so amazing and your dynamics will bloom magnificently. You will have a knowing that will develop from this retrospection that will be an important part of you for the rest of your life.

At the end of the exercise, you are going to take everything you recognized in that retrospection and say, "O.K. God, here are all the good things and not-so-good things that happened in my day. Here's the great me and the not-so-great me. Take it all, gather it all together and cleanse it for me. Wash it for me, scrub it, launder it and put it into its place so I can see how it turns out the next day." Watch what happens with all the feelings you had when you were going through these events. They will be completely different because the entire essence of it is changed. Every aspect of it has been purified for you and is changed. This is the Retrospective exercise.

Practice it without telling anyone else what you are doing. It may take only five or ten minutes to complete at first, but as you continue with the exercise you will see how simple and swift it becomes. The events become clearer and clearer in your mind.

Be objective when doing this exercise. If you find yourself getting emotional, say, "OK God, here's another thing. My emotion is interfering here. Wash it, cleanse it, and heal it. Give it back to me when you've done the laundry." Only cover one day in each exercise. Start every day anew.

This is not a confession of so-called negative events. It represents all events from one day; All conversations, all significant events from that single day.

Sleep is a totally regenerative process. It is an important part of your growth and development. If you find you want to take twenty or thirty-minute nap on the weekend (or whichever days constitute your weekend), do it. It can be very restorative and refreshing. Just remember not to take the nap too late in the day or it will interfere with your nighttime sleep process.

Part X: Frequently Asked Questions

Q: Breathing Question: Are we supposed to be concentrating on breathing in through the nostrils and out through the mouth just to get into this state or are we supposed to be breathing like this the whole time we are meditating?

A: This type of breathing is conducive to throwing you into the meditative state. It's a pattern that was established eons ago. It will help you. And then you will find yourself breathing so slightly, you won't even think there is a breath in your body that's happening. Don't get hung up on breathing.

Q: When I meditate I feel a tremendous pressure inside my head, what is this?

A: This pressure is not a headache. It is a developmental process that is happening within your sight. This is something that happens when you are becoming more aware. It represents that your sight is opening up again.

Mystics throughout the ages have referred to "The Eye" as sand, which over eons of time evolves into glass. It keeps developing and growing. What's happening is that you, in particular, are going through a transformational process. Something is developing within you and your body is adapting to it. It is a process and will continue for the rest of your life. You have shown the Self inside your willingness to go through this change, so the pressure you feel happens automatically. To some, it is a minor, discomforting feeling. To most, it's like an internal massage, welcoming and comfortable. Enjoy it!

Q: I saw only black while I was meditating -- what does this mean? Is it something bad?

A: This is a big misconception. Everyone thinks that black is bad, that it's death. Black is really the embryonic fluid, the breeding ground within the mind of God. It is the utmost essence where the seed of thought is planted. It's the breeding ground in God. The greatest nature of all color. Black is good. Black is not bad. There is no good or bad. That is only our perception.

Q: What should we do with our eyes while they are closed? Do we look up?

A: Your eyes will go up naturally as you go within. You should not have to force them to this position. This is a natural and automatic process of going within.

Q: I have the hardest time sitting still. Why is this?

A: Your body is adapting to a more relaxed state and is not used to it. You have a lot of energy in you that must adjust to this still-natured state. Hang in there. Be observant of these things, but every time you feel these discomforts, let them flow away as if they are going down a drain.

Q: I only see colors when I meditate. Is this O.K.?

A: These colors are serving a purpose. Colors carry consciousness, a vibrational frequency of understanding and perception that carries information. This information is translated into our super subconscious for adaptation into a form we can relate to in our consciousness. Colors represent that you are on a stepping-stone heading toward realization in its understanding. The act of perceiving only colors will fade after a while and other impressions will follow.

Q: I get nothing when I meditate.

A: Keep at it. You really are receiving something, but you are not letting go enough to perceive it consciously. Practice, expect nothing, and you will begin to see more and know more.

Q: When I meditate I see people I don't know. Who are they?

A: When this happens, just let it flow. If there is a specific message you are to receive, you will know. Just keep flowing with whatever you get, but as I talked about this earlier, always challenge it.

Creator

Chapter 5

Intuition, Awareness and Knowing

Creator

" Without the recognition of Self love, how can we truly help another to love or even feel better, unless we can truly begin to love ourselves?"

Creator

Part I: Develop your Conscious Awareness.

In order to develop your *intuitive awareness* of Self we must first discuss Conscious Awareness. Conscious Awareness is the act of being consciously aware of what is going on around you and within you, relating either to the conversation or actions around and/or within you. In developing your intuitive skills, you must be able to control and stop yourself and consciously become aware of what is happening.

Exercise in Conscious Awareness.

As an example, try this exercise for one minute. Sit quietly and think of nothing. Now, notice all the conversations you're having in your mind. I want you to consciously stop yourself from any of these conversations. Stop yourself from being wrapped up in your conversation. Just watch yourself. Stop the thinking process that is wrapped up in that conversation. Stop your thought process and see what is really being said and what is really being done. Next, watch yourself as another person talks. Try it for just one minute. Concentrate on what is really happening. This is all that is needed, one minute in your life. You will notice how busy and active things seem around you. You may think you have no control over what one says, or what one thinks. Think again. We can actually stop our thoughts in their tracks. We can decide whether we want to think (or say or do) that specific thought (or word or action.) We can change it any time we want, that is our free will. You will soon become aware that one minute does not, in actuality, have a specific time element or duration. Actually, there is no time in the non-linear world.

Here is another exercise in conscious awareness: Watch what is really being said and done around and within you. Now, think of your Self inside, not the "little" you but the "big" Self that resides inside. Totally surrender to Self. Constantly love it and let it know you love it. Feel its constant warmth and flow. Now watch and feel the scene of the conversation. Unbeknownst to you, you will be taken into this process of expanded awareness and you will be able to tune into a new, more real conscious awareness. With this experience, over time, your times of dramas and traumas will fade away. What was your experience? Reflect for a moment on your experience with this exercise.

The more often you practice this simple exercise, the greater effect it will have in your life which has previously been so full of reactions and disappointments. You will begin to experience a sense of relative indifference to those old dramas, the situations to which you previously reacted. Now, with your heart and soul, feel the love coming into you. It is your new clothing. Consciously talk to It from inside your head, there's no need to talk out loud, and realize that it is a close friend. In becoming aware, you will pick up more. You will realize more, you will know more. That is what awareness is. You are taking it on; you are clothing yourself in it.

Think of your Self inside. Love it constantly and let it know you love It. Feel the warmth and flow of it. It flows constantly. Now as you watch what is really happening within and around you, there is a shift.

Unbeknownst to you, you will be taken into this process and you will be able to tune into a new, more real conscious awareness.

Part II: Conscious Prayer with Every Thought, Word and Action

This discussion is worth repeating. The root and basis of everything I teach is based on prayer because I am conscious of it. Here is my understanding of the concept of Prayer.

> *"As you think, so you are. Every word, every thought, every action is your living prayer."*

As we live and interact in the world, we find ourselves praying in one or all of three ways: mentally, through our perceptions and thoughts; vocally, through our words; and actively, through our chosen actions. It is such that our thoughts are absolutely made manifest as effects of our prayer. What we want is what we get. There is an expression, "Be careful what you wish for, it will come true." Think about it.

We can pray to negate or affirm something. Everything is prayer, and we have free choice as to how we utilize our prayers. If someone tells you they wish ill for you, though, it will not manifest unless you also choose to believe them and accept this prayer. You have the choice not to accept anything of this nature. Isn't that a great thing to know?

What you accept is what you get

Be consciously aware of what is happening with you and around you. It is then that you will feel something happening within you and your resistance to accepting what you perceive will be diminished. Be as totally in that consciousness as you can. Be in that Godliness that is giving Itself to you. Get yourself out of the way. Keep practicing. Do you understand the importance of practice by now? Talk to this consciousness as if to a close friend. It will have more to give you as you become more comfortable with it. And you will begin to pick up more insight and knowing. You will get impressions. Don't ignore or dismiss them. You are now open to these things.

Remember, mass mind is what we've learned in life. Its basis is fear and mistrust, and its purpose is to keep you as a part of it. Until now you have been taught and understand that as long as you believe what everyone else believes, you then can feel a sense of "belonging" with the rest of the population. In fact, mass mind is keeping you from the truth – this truth is not based on fear and mistrust, but on faith and knowing.

The mass mind understanding of the ego is that it gives glorification to us. The ego is an innate tool to bring us glorification. It makes us feel strong, confident and secure in our world. Mass mind believes this glorification should be put down. Many of the "New Agers" agree that we must get rid of the ego. My understanding is that the ego is a necessary part of us. It is not the cause of our inability or reluctance to let go of issues within us. There are causal events, which precipitated the distress in our lives. We cannot blame the ego, but what causes the ego to swell. This must be clearly understood; the ego has a purpose and function. It is to allow the Godliness to express itself in glorification and humility. We are the ones who have distorted it. This explains what the ego really is and what its purpose is in our lives.

Part III: Awareness Is Your Tool

Here is one example of awareness kicking in without being necessarily conscious of it. Have you noticed how, once you have found your love in your life, all sorts of people from your past start coming out again? Do you know why? They start contacting you again because somewhere inside themselves they have become aware that something has been done to increasingly sever their ties to you.

Another example: You are planning to do a simple task while you are busy with other events in your life. As you have temporarily forgotten about that task, you see that it no longer needs to be done because someone else is fulfilling it. It was in their mind to complete this task, too. Maybe you were picking up on their consciousness, or they were picking up on yours. Many things like this happen. No doubt you have plentiful examples of your own. This is shared awareness.

Awareness becomes your tool. Accept whatever it is that you become aware of. Do not dismiss this tool. If you are having a thought about something or someone, you must believe its truth. Even if we don't get to express the perfection, or if the perfection is not being totally expressed to us in some way, our perception needs to be objective without being tainted with judgment. This is how we find the understanding of our perception. Even when the other person may deny what you are perceiving. Use your intuitive awareness. Practice with it. Hone this tool, make it a strong presence in your conscious life.

Practice the exercise: Be aware of what is happening around you and within you. Step out of yourself. It is as if you are talking to someone else when

118

you step out of yourself. Continue with what you were doing or saying, but watch what is happening. Practice it.

Recently, my friend Rich approached me to help him with perception. I gave him the following story as a dynamic exercise to practice to strengthen perception.

In 1974, while I lived in Boston, I was walking downtown with another member of the Order, Sr. Rebecca. We were having a discussion about sight. She was trying to explain to me how we are able to "see" via the act of perceiving. She instructed me to focus on a fellow who was approaching us from a block away. She then asked me to immediately use my perception and tell her what his life was like. Before I could interject to tell her that I didn't know how to do this, I found myself perceiving and understanding this man's life and was able to express this aloud to her. I didn't stop expressing what I suddenly "knew" about his life until he was about five feet in front of us. She turned to me and said, "Good!" That was my first experience with using perception to see. It is a wonderful tool. Remember, Self is not incorrect. Try it. Trust it.

Part IV: Everything Is There for Our Purpose

Everything is OK; everything that happens in our life happens for a purpose. Everything is a stepping stone.

Once when I was in Fort Worth, Br. Doug and I were walking in an area known for its slaughterhouses. The streets were mostly empty. We were walking on the sidewalk, which was fairly wide, along the block filled with storefronts. The sidewalk intersected with a very odd-looking alley. I knew from walking this neighborhood, that there was nothing in this alley; no doors to the stores, no windows, no entrances or exits at all. The alley was U-shaped, with two blank brick walls on both sides, and another wall in back, forming the "U". There was only one way out; that was on our street side. Like I said, it was an odd alley.

Before we reached the alley, we saw an emaciated street bum standing by a parking meter next to the street. His face was covered with oozing cuts, as if a razor had been taken to his face. His glazed eyes were tinted yellow. His clothing was oily, dirty and tattered. I walked up to him and said, "Oh my God, you're hurt! Can I help you?" Doug said, "Let's get out of here. Let's go!" I said, "No!" The guy looked at me, but didn't answer me. I repeated my request to let me help him and he finally responded very simply, by shaking his head "no." I insisted that he let me help him. I said, "I'm going to help you." The cuts on his face were awful. So I put my hands up in front of his face. He immediately backed away from me and ducked into the alley only a couple of feet away.

When the street bum disappeared from view, we heard a horrible sound coming from the alley. It was a high-pitched scream, but it wasn't like a human's scream, it was much higher than a human voice could reach. I went to look in the alley and the guy was not there.

I then realized that this was a learning experience, a set up for me. I know that everything is put in front of us as a stepping stone for our growth. It's real. Everything. There is nothing to be afraid of, no darkness, no shadow can stand in the light. None. This was the lesson I took with me from this experience.

Creator

Chapter 6

Understanding Healing

Creator

124

"As we cannot destroy matter, nor can we destroy the memories of the non-linear. We can only rearrange it to a different consciousness."

Creator

Healing is simply this:

We can utilize our Self, as It utilizes us, and our *inner sight* to focus on something and help It to realize Its perfection. We are then taking something and recreating It as a newer and greater consciousness. Using energy and light as tools to recreate change, we can take negative energy and shift it into a more positive, focused and productive form of energy.

When referring to energy from this point forward, I am talking about what quantum physics refers to as morphic fields. As I understand them, morphic fields contain information that can be initiated, created and manifested. If this is true, then every one of us has the ability to recreate healing within ourselves and with others.

In this chapter, I will incorporate a mildly esoteric understanding to help you break more deeply into the reality of the healing world. You will gain purposeful and useful information through these exercises that will enable you to realize your source of energy and its causes, which can be purposefully directed in either a creative or destructive livingness. You will gain knowledge of your individual source of insight and learn how to utilize the ability of Its energy used in healing not only within yourself, but for the benefit of others as well.

Try to remember that healing naturally affects you, whether you are working on yourself or others. I am presenting healing techniques and exercises to aid in your developing awareness of energy and light. These ancient exercises have been used for thousands of years and have influenced humankind in the developmental process to find the Divinity/Godliness within.

Part I: Introduction to Healing: Using Your Inner Insight and Imagination as a Tool

We're going to talk about imagination and how to change something through visualization in order to create, and recreate, something newer or greater. We use "image in action" as a tool to create a newer, better idea or thing. In order to do this we have to see "It" in its perfection -- the way we believe it's supposed to be in its final, perfect form. If we cannot visualize this, healing is not going to be accomplished.

Nothing is really "new;" It's just been further developed

For example, someone invented a chair. Someone else added wheels to it to make it a "rolling" chair. Then another person wanted it to be more comfortable and added arms, and another added a back to rest against. Take a look at everything around you and reflect on its ongoing developmental stages. Everything is developed into something more or greater than it started out. Therefore, there really is nothing new in this universe. Everything is in continual manifestation and re-creation. Everything has a definite pattern, form and shape into which it is transformed. If we can understand this, we can also understand the development process of health, developing this into what becomes our ultimate goal.

Read the next few passages with care so you gain further understanding. In this concept of development, we can reframe what already exists and is applicable to our own developmental process in the mental and emotional arenas of our lives. This includes everything pertaining to our life that has brought us to the place that we are today and where we will be tomorrow.

Understanding this perspective, we can now also understand that tomorrow doesn't exist. Tomorrow is actually now and therefore the "tomorrow" concept is, in fact, our own limitation in our developmental process. This is what healing is based upon. Call this a presumption if you choose, but then this too becomes a limitation because you then do not hold this concept as a definite knowable understanding. The definite knowable understanding is "knowing and accepting." That is healing. Healing is based only on our world of knowing and accepting.

When we live within our limitations and accept those limitations, we cannot be healed of that which we are working. It is our goal to search, to find, and to release any and all limitations so we can then be truly healed.

Given this, we now know that we have the ability to imagine how to make a better product or a better way of doing something. Once we have imagined it, or created an "image in action" (for that is what we are doing, seeing something in what we think is its perfect form,) once we tap into our Self as a resource to re-form our source, as a re-formation, we will then be shown how to achieve this visualized image.

We will get an idea from Self of what its final form is. Self speaks of this in formations of words and images. We will be shown an idea. This idea is likened to a point of light with images of information within it made manifest in the darkness (our ignorance), in the depths of blackness which represent the breeding ground of Godliness within us. This is where all things first manifest. This light carries a world of information for us to draw upon. This information arises from sources embedded within our experience and wisdom. It will seem ironic that just as you are focusing on something, thinking about how to make it better, an idea will come to you. If you can feel it for a moment, it feels like inspiration or euphoria.

Self is intuitive, the Source inside you

"Intuitive" means inner teaching. So we will get this idea from Self, but then we think, "Oh! I've got it!" and then we have a tendency to claim it as though it was us who designed it. It wasn't us, it was this individualized "Self," this inner sight intelligence inside showing you what your something is going to look like or what it should sound like or feel like or could be like. This is our golden opportunity to acknowledge Self. We haven't seen the image before our eyes because it has yet to be manifested. We don't see it in front of us, because we see it inside as an impression, when it isn't yet tangible, as a greater idea. But it will become manifested as we step out on it. Even if we create the physicality of it, this physical manifestation is not, and never could be, the actual perfection It knows, but only the image of perfection we think it could be. We try to get to the closest point of perfection, yet we will fall short. Only Self

131

knows the true image of perfection. We must trust this knowing and follow its lead as if we were blind.

In this way, we have inner sight. We have the ability to create and co-create in Its image. If this is true, then we truly are co-creators in Its (His/Her) image. Get the idea yet? This is huge stuff.

We have the ability to recreate something greater in Its image

Keep this in mind. It is one of the greatest keys to understanding, in fact, one of the greatest keys ever known to the human race:

Again: We have the ability to re-create something greater in its image

In our life, we have been taught to settle for what "is," what has been shown to "be." The fact is we do not have to continue to accept these things. These things are just what we have been taught and what we have accepted. This "accepted-as-the-norm" thought or action is only the beginning of what can be. We can go beyond this and be open to the synchronistic flow of life and actually recreate what has been shown to us already. Once we become aware of this possibility, we become a greater participant in the synchronistic flow of life. Too few human beings on earth realize and grasp this conceptual truth. To review, we can image a goal in its final form and actually express it, build it, and create it. This is worth repeating.

We can image a goal in its final form and actually internalize it, create it and manifest it

Every one of us has a unique ability and a unique capacity of working with healing. Everyone has a different personality aspect and a different way to utilize healing energy and healing light that emits from within. You will learn which way is your way as there is an aspect of healing energy and/or healing light that is your unique style of knowing.

Part II: The Law and The Truth in Action

There is something called the law and the truth. This is another aspect of the basis for what I refer to as healing and other gifts. A person does not heal oneself nor anyone else. The law and the truth do via the Divinity within, the God within, Self or whatever you want to call It. As we begin to trust and accept that It knows what It is doing, it begins to have an effect in our lives and the lives of others. Our place is to get out of the way and allow it to happen. Once we give It direction, with intent, It knows what to do without our interference. But the rub is that we must allow Its power, force and energy to take over. We must get out of the way.

It is written that we are created in Its (His/Her) image. We have said that we have the ability to recreate. We also have free will and can freely and willfully destroy ourselves daily in our dramas and traumas, if we so choose. Previously we thought we had no choice in this, but we do. These dramas and traumas are the sabotages of daily-learned living, the "conversations" we have been taught, have accepted and lived with all our lives.

Trust that the Divinity is alive and well within us. It is with us every moment of our lives. We all have this Voice within us. It is the light that is alive. It is of pure consciousness, and it has pure untainted intelligence.

Healing is a universal principal, a law, which states that "what we accept, so we get"

Every thought is a causal moment, either consciously or subconsciously, but always leads to its effect. It's the law of cause and effect, for every action (or thought) there is an equal and opposite reaction. What you sow is what you reap. And so on.

An Israeli university has proven that thinking can create movement and reaction. Remember the times when you were walking down a street focusing on some thought process and all of a sudden you turn around because you think or feel someone or something is right behind you? When you turn around quickly, what you find is they are actually some distance away, but staring at you. You are picking up on a vibrational pattern, a frequency.

Science has proven through various studies that our thoughts provide a physical energy and can really produce activity and can actually be measured with proper instrumentation. An analogy of this would be that we are a camera that is taking a picture and actually creating a movement because of that impression, because the impression then manifests. There are some people who, with a camera, can engage in a mental visual of an image that is not in front of them. This image then appears on the negative of the film. This being true, we can proceed to the next level of thought whereby if we are working on someone in healing, we can hold an impression of that which we perceive as its perfection, and that person will be affected by this impression.

The law of cause and effect is a constant in the flow of life

You will find all sorts of application of this in life, not only with healing but included in your everyday life. You can find its validity by becoming more of a participant in your life. Pay attention to what you are thinking, or knowing, then look around and pay attention to what you encounter next. Don't you always run into the exact person you are trying to avoid? Don't you hear from the person you were just thinking about? There are endless applications of this principle in action. What were you thinking? How does that relate to what happens next? Then what happens? Learn to trust yourself. It is everything. Becoming more aware of these principals and watching objectively for their effects, without your ingrained sabotages. These causes and effects occur consistently within our immediate world, within the world around us and finally with all the people who are affected in our world for generations to come. Isn't that exciting!

Take the gesture we use daily of waving to someone to say hello. In ancient Hebraic time, the right hand was the hand of blessing. So when you hold up your right hand to say hello, you are, historically speaking, asking a blessing for that person. This may be a reflective and a reciprocated action to us, yet it is actually based on ancient history, a pattern established from a ritual that has been taught and passed down through the generations of all people. It is a ritual that's in action within the mind. It's always being recreated every day. The person you are waving to, saying hello or good-bye to, without any realization on their part, will feel something inside for that moment. They and we will feel camaraderie, they'll feel an essence of something that they can relate to but cannot or will not express.

Tune in to your intuition

We can tune in to ourselves, build awareness and utilize the intuition that is associated within that very moment of response. It is the moment of discovery.

Think of all the times when people would approach you and even though they did not express it, you knew they felt good with you, safe with you, and trusted you. What they are going through at that moment is what you perceive from them. It is actually what is happening in them and their life to create what we see in that moment. We can see the dramas and traumas, the sadness, the joy, the pain or something more on their mind. We can sense this through perception. You can sense through perception of pictures in the moment. Do you want to know something pertaining to that person? Then ask yourself within, and an intuitional idea or thought will come to you in the flash of the moment and it will be correct. If you were to ask them they might admit what you confront them with, but only if their feeling and thinking aren't fear based. Otherwise, if their constitution is based on fear, and they are trying to fool the world, they won't admit their emotional conversation. You can learn to apply this intuitive use of the law throughout your life.

Part III: Genetic Code:
An Important Concept

The soul is the path of experience. This is our record of history and exists only as our path of experience. The soul is always searching externally for guidance from the more physical or scientific realm of our lives. Every experience is stored in the neural receptors that make up our body's response. They are then carried in a memory of what I refer to as genetic code.

At night, when we are asleep and out of the way, we have up to three billion neurological responses happening within us. Each one carries a little piece of what we are going to be experiencing from that moment on into the next day and for the rest of our lives. (So much for free will as we know it.) As far-fetched as this may seem, this is actually forming a pattern, a shape of thought, of what our responses are turning into. It's a pattern that is yet to be manifested. This activity is the formation of events yet to occur. There are numerous pathways and concoctions that may appear, according to our experience. It happens consistently throughout our time of sleep. This is one reason that sleep is so important in our lives. The more things we have going on in our dynamical lives, the more things are to be created in a form that in turn creates what we are going to be doing tomorrow, what we are thinking, feeling, our perceptions, our responses, our actions, everything.

Though some may call these dynamics acts of fate, I refer to them as free will because through our free will, we determine which path we will be traveling. Our paths are constantly changing and flowing and leading to everything else. We can actually hear our thoughts and the directions we are heading toward, which thoughts we are discounting and which we pay attention to, but we need sleep to help work these images through.

This warrants further explanation as it is a vital part of understanding healing and every person's ability to create healing for themselves and for others.

Genetic code relates to the relationship between events and synchronicity

Everything is in the mind of God; our mind is also within the mind of God, and people reciprocate in response to this relationship with God. When patterns get set up with reactions, it takes the first form as a mental reaction. Using myself as an example: I set it up and I accept it in one way or many ways, but always on some conscious level. In other words, we have an atmosphere that emanates from within us and that we live within. This atmosphere is electrically charged with activity of known and unknown formations.

This atmosphere becomes externalized and is filled within the mind, the mind of God that we live within and that lives within us. We are physically made of electrical bodies presented in a concentrated, semi-dense, formed mass. This mass has electrically charged emanations that carry intent of constant information that we have recreated from our conversations and perceptions of experiences and the things that are taught to us in our subconscious state. These emanations of intent carry a pattern. The culmination of the pattern is the substance of a consciousness that manifests in our world and atmosphere around us and influences the universe as patterns are set up for the next event. This is the etheric substance that manifests as the next scene emanates forth in "unbeknownst consciousness" from us in a pre set-up pattern that we actually pre-manifested!

Concerning our recognition of Self: we are coming more of age referring to the bridge between the linear and non-linear world of thought. This also refers to the bridge between the linear/non-linear time/event of our evolutionary process of and in all life. It is our process of coming home. It is also the recognition of who we are, what we are and why we are today. The function of the ego is to express who we really are, and not the way we have been taught to be. It pertains to coming back to our truer Self, as in the parable of the prodigal Son (sun).

Part IV: Purest Definition of "Disease": How Emotional, Physiological Patterns become Established in a Person.

All emotional trauma of the past is held in the cells of the body in the form of energy. The trauma is the creation of the disease body. It starts with our mental perceptions and then moves into our emotional response and how we accept it.

When an event occurs in your life, whether you participate actively or observe an event, you take it in and it affects you emotionally. As an example, we may not be aware of how we are going to react the first time we experience something, but then we figure out how we think we are supposed to feel, and what we should do about it. Perhaps we will cry or feel hurt. And then, over the years, every time some similar situation or scenario occurs, we learn to react to it even more or hold it in and it becomes an ingrained memory and "re-action."

In this ingrained memory, the reaction becomes a pattern within us and every aspect of our lives reacts in regard to this. And so on. It begins to leak throughout us and becomes a part of our personality and behavior. Perhaps we learn that we should not cry, perhaps we learn we will be yelled at or hit or mocked throughout our lives. Perhaps we learn that we are owed much more than the world gives us. Whatever it is, it carries through every aspect of how we live our life.

In the next step, these reactions bleed into us on a biological level and this begins to take on the manifestation of psychological disease (the inflammation of irritations). Over the years we continue to ignore the lessons to be learned. These memories take on the actual physical manifestation of a disease state and we become physically challenged.

This is what you are feeling when you are working to heal another person. Emotional traumas of the past are held in the cells of the body. I call it the remembrance, which is held in the cells. We feel this in the form of energy. When this trauma is released through healing, we are working on it and we must wait until we feel the flow of its release.

Sometimes the other person will not feel the change at first, or they will feel it sometime in the next day or two. You have to know and trust it is done based on your experience in feeling, witnessing the release. You will know. Once it is done, whether it is you or another person, you will realize that the old patterns diminish and your life is in the process of changing.

I have found that events which happen during a difficult birthing process can be linked to physical manifestations. For example, if a baby is delivered by metal forceps, this then changes the cranial rhythm of the baby and this is a strain, stress and irritation that will affect them for their entire lives. This can be repaired in order to spare that person unnecessary physical problems in their life, if you can find one of the few doctors of osteopathy that practice the understanding of the spiritual-psychical world of healing.

What is disease?

The law knows nothing about disease. Disease is nothing but a mental picture to be eradicated by clear thinking. Very few diseases are inherited. Most people are subjected to diseases at the ages of one thru seven, pre-birth or in the birthing process. Take asthma, one situation and dilemma. It is not a hereditary disease. There are many people I have worked with who had asthmatic conditions as well as lung, throat, jaw and mouth problems. Through my work, I have found that the majority of these people had clamps or forceps used during the birthing process. They might not have been properly spanked. Perhaps not enough air was allowed to come forth to create their first cry. People I have worked on have asked their mothers or another immediate family member who was present at the time, so this has been verified over and over by many people. I also know that we can create, almost like a circulation in the lungs, a life force flowing through that will help this condition. There are others with asthmatic conditions that have had their breath taken from them in shock or extreme dismay and subsequently developed breathing, throat or lung distresses. We can work with these situations to help them become better.

In your own way, you can focus your attention and concentration to feel healing according to your unique ability. As in my "The Art of Healing" seminars, you will understand the potential of what the power, force and energy of this consciousness can actually accomplish in our world and the world around us.

You will be presented several exercises in the next section to learn to focus on the art of healing and how it feels for you. You will understand what your unique ability is.

Part V: Realize Your Place in Healing

It is our place to listen in humility when we are working with healing. In fact, it is our place to listen at all times. We are living healers. We carry it with us wherever we go, even when we are sleeping. You just have to become more conscious of it. You don't have to let anyone know that you are more conscious of it, but you can tell someone that you know that you can be of help.

You can learn to listen in an objective way, not participating in reaction. You can learn to speak in a way to show you can comprehend someone else's distress. You can then see the results of your listening. This alone will be helpful in helping others achieve better balance. When you are listening in some way, the silence will bring them an answer in some form.

There are those who will approach you in a hostile, rather negative way. The only purpose of that is to negate or sabotage you and throw you off. It is the same as when you are feeling really strong about something and someone comes along and says or does something that bumps you away from that feeling. Your euphoria is in the consciousness of the atmosphere that you carry, and that other person is only there to try to throw you off balance and help you to sabotage yourself. They are successful only if you allow it to happen. Easy theory to understand, yet takes practice to master.

Remember, when you are listening to someone, help them disassociate from the problem and redirect them. Help them to realize that at any moment they can choose again. They will understand this. Help them to realize this and make another choice. A cliché that I have enjoyed is that we have the ability to make lemonade out of a lemon.

You can use your ability any time you want. If you don't use it all the time, don't feel guilty. It's waiting for the time when you do use it. Then that becomes the practice time for the next time. Everything is practice. You will then be in a learning mode, and you can always continue to grow.

It is not your job to "heal the world." There are so many contributing factors in our lives, and it is not necessarily our place to work with everyone. You may not be the right person to work with an individual, and they may not need to have your "help." There may be someone else, according to their acceptance of what they want and need to accept in life, that may be better suited to achieve one person's needs than you are. This is absolutely fine. There are all kinds of scenarios. I don't recommend that you lay this ability on all sorts of other people at random. Today's world is much more accepting of healing than it was even five years ago. It will continue to grow in acceptance. If someone is interested in what you have to offer, go for it. Reach out, step up, and go for it!

Part VI: Healing: Where To Begin. Feeling the Light and Feeling the Energy

There is a flow of magnetic energy that flows across the body. This flow follows the heat cycle and, if we become really still, we can feel the pulse of the flow of this cycle. When I am working with someone, one of my own indicators is feeling this pulse, this flow. When I feel the flow moving freely, I know the healing for that area is completed. The other person may feel the effects either immediately or over time, whatever is needed for them. But I know the seed has been planted. It has been fertilized and now it will start to develop. It might need a reminder every now and then according to the sabotage (which we will discuss in detail later) the recipient experiences. When we remind it, the consciousness of the dynamic will change.

Following are several exercises so you can realize what it is you "feel" when tuned into the magnetic energy of a body. They are healing-concentration exercises and some require the use of a partner. Be quiet, be still, fully tune in to what you experience.

Breathing through your nose and out gently through your mouth is breathing in the breath of God. Do this and feel the sensation in your head. Concentrate on your breathing and notice a change in how you feel. You will feel a clarity, something you did not feel before. This simple act of concentration on your breathing can create productive changes that will stay with you the rest of your life.

Exercise 1: Grounding Exercise

Here is an exercise that is good for you to practice to experience what the healing energy feels like to you. This exercise also happens to be helpful for those with moderate dyslexia and it's good for calming an emotionally chaotic state, or an over-stimulated state, what I sometimes refer to as a "bombarded mind." Here is a "grounding exercise."

The pads of our fingers act as terminals which transmit a current. They also are receivers for current. The first three fingers, the thumb, forefinger and the middle finger, carry the greatest current. You can "feel" through the fingertips. A lot of nerve endings are located here for that purpose. What I've done with this exercise in the past seems to help relieve others of their feelings of chaos and confusion. When I've taught this exercise in the past, it helps many people understand what energy and light feel like.

The left hand is a receiver. The right hand is a transmitter. Historically, you gesture hello with the right hand. You are sending or transmitting a blessing to that person. The right hand is the giving hand, the left hand receives. In this exercise, take your right hand and hold the first two fingers about one inch apart and gently place them about one to one and a half inches above the eyebrows. You'll notice there are two slight indentations on your forehead where they seem to naturally fit. You can do this anytime, anywhere. Barely touch your forehead in with these fingers. If you leave your fingers there for a little while, you will begin to feel a slight sensation in your fingers and/or in your head that would build up and then disperse. You are dispersing chaotic energy. The effect you get depends on your needs at that moment. Sometimes it takes five seconds to complete, sometimes a little longer.

I've heard a lot of good things from many people regarding how effective it is for them. It's not an anchor re-set, as they call it in the fields of psychology and sociology, but something that has great effect. It's almost like finding a comfortable spot an inch and a half above your eyebrows and an inch and a half apart. Remember, you just barely touch this spot with your fingers.

The sensation you feel is the stimulation of a neurological response. Again, it's great for the mildly dyslexic person, or if you are burning out at home or work and you feel like you can't handle things very well. It's almost like an ignition start and may feel like a flickering of a candle. It stimulates something inside your skull. Esoterically speaking, there is a place between the pituitary and pineal glands inside your head called an "arc." Life is there. In a fully functioning human being, that arc is fully ignited. If the arc is not there, then the person's life is listless, and quickly deteriorating, or they are not alive and breathing. There will be times, though, when the arc is fluctuating or sputtering, when there is less emotional and physical function in the person. You can stimulate that arc and its path when you do this exercise. You feel much better when the arc is functioning at its capacity.

Exercise 2: Five-Finger Exercise

This is a simple exercise that allows us to feel the energy, the light, the presence of the Divinity Within. Again as you begin this exercise, your hands and fingers will be barely touching. There is no need to rub your hands together to gather an electrical charge. Simply place the five fingers from each hand together in a make-shift tent. You can have them up or down, but don't let your hands touch silk or wool because that will create an unnecessary discharge and diminish the effect of the exercise. Don't press your fingers together, barely hold them there. Then hold this position until you feel the full effect.

You'll notice a feeling of heat or vibrational sensation between the palms even if you have cold hands. Notice how it begins to build. It will increase. The palms will begin to tingle a little bit and more life force will flow into the blood. Wait there until you feel the flow in your fingers or your hands. Actually, you are assisting the life force and its flow. Your hands can be up or down, whatever is comfortable for you.

This exercise not only provides a greater neural flow and sensitivity and stimulus, but improves the flow of the life force which flows through you. This will affect your day, and your entire life. What you are feeling is not because of a blood pressure change, though it will affect your blood pressure. People who have their hands down near their lap, or straight out in front, are also feeling this.

This exercise will help during the day if you are not feeling well, if you are shaking, or feeling a lot of chaos in your day. This will help eliminate that. It will help you feel better inside. If you feel stuffy in your head, this will help. A lot of these things help in our life if we just apply these simple things. There is nothing to them, they are easy and so beneficial for us.

Exercise 3: Energy-Stabilizing Exercise

To complete this exercise, you will need a partner. Stand up facing one another.

Take hold of the other person's hand. Cross your arms so you are holding your right hand with their left hand, and your left with their right hand. Relax and close your eyes. Breathe in very slowly. Breathe in through your nose all the way down to your belly and gently and slowly out through your mouth. No heavy breathing. No hyperventilating. Slow and easy. Feel a lightness filling in your head. I want you to become aware of your partner's size, their shape and their temperature. Try to tune into that world, just for a moment. Now begin to feel the energy flow between you as you are becoming more one with that person, less threatened by that person. Really get into it. Concentrate on the energy flow between each of you, become one with it. The less resistance, the less threat, the less fear, the greater the flow. Let it flow. There is nothing to be afraid of.

Try to get in touch with the energy pull of that flow, of that energy called gravity. And in that you will feel the weight of its magnetism. It's a flow that is being established. Let it come into you. Don't restrict it. Feel it flowing freely. Tap into that flow a little bit. Open the bottom of your feet as if they are vents and allow the earth's gravity to enter you. See it, imagine it, feel it as a flow melting through you, flowing up through you like lava, in to your muscles, your bones and nerves. The vents in your feet will open up wider and wider. Feel the weight of it, the raw power of it. Let it flow up through your ankles, your lower legs. It might feel uncomfortable at first, bear it out. It will break through finally. Your knees, going up into your thighs, your hips, settling in your belly or lower back. Now feel it flow up through your chest and upper back and shoulders. It's a flow. It's magnetic. Let it flow through your arms and elbows. There are little logjams it will break through. Let it flow through your forearms, your wrists, your fingers, your hands. Let it break through. Nothing can stop it. And finally into your partner's fingers. Now that the flow is started, notice your breathing. How slow it is, how soft it is. Slowly open up your eyes.

This is a very exciting and useful exercise. It is a healing concentration for the elimination of various bone, liver and skull ailments. You'll find it different every time you use it. Especially for the person that you are using it with. Even if you have never seen them before and you do it with a new person each time. Each person will always find it helping them according to their own needs.

Over the years, I have used this exercise in my seminars on the Art of Healing. Interestingly, there have been many responses to this exercise in terms of what people sensed or felt. Here are a few of the more frequently related responses.

Susie: "I was totally relaxed, I could feel the flow circulate through us."

Judy: "I felt so calm. My headache totally dissipated."

Gina: "My head was just throbbing and as you were talking about our feet opening up as vents, I felt myself wanting to cry because I felt I had to trust my partner and then I opened myself up to trusting people, which is so new for me."

Art: "I felt a vibration in our palms, it was real warm, and I could feel a rhythm."

Kathy: "My leg muscles were really shaking, and I'm very, very hot right now."

Jill: "All of a sudden, I felt like I was very heavy, leaning to the left. I felt we were both leaning and I was going to fall over." (Mark: "That's actually the magnetic force which is throwing you into a balance of what you were and what your potential could be, too.")

Healing means finding the source of distress, then letting it go so you can move on

In healing, if we can become still, we will receive a flash of intuition and that is when we will know what the source of distress is. Recognize what the source was, and then let it go so you (or others) can move on in life. If you trust It, then you can let It do Its job and you can let go. Easy to say, but it takes practice. Practice. Practice. Practice. You can do this with yourself and others. Sometimes the situation will have already been worked out but the body is still feeling the effects of it. In this case, hold onto that spot and wait until you feel the energy flow freely. Follow your intuition and it will guide you. No harm can come from healing. But, we're getting ahead of ourselves, let's get down to business.

Creator

Chapter 7

Healing: Getting Started

Creator

156

*"No Darkness, no Shadow
can stand in the Light."*

Creator

Part I: Focus in Healing

I work under the assumption of knowing and accepting that we are all healers. Each of us has the ability and capability to "listen" to that voice within each of us. That voice is an idea, it is clear. It is consciousness of purity itself and It has intelligence to know what to do with or without our help of expression...as long as we are in the reference of "giving."

It is our place to listen purposefully when working with other people. In healing, we place our hands near or on someone. While we do this, we are allowing the Voice and Its clarity to take over.   And It does so without judgment nor condemnation. Without our interference, It knows what needs to be done or to happen and what does not need to happen or be done.

While working with someone, if we find ourselves with a judgement of what we want to change in the other person, then we have just negated ourselves, sabotaged our Self and our prayer of being able to help. The trick is to allow the healing to happen without us getting in the way.   As the expression goes, "Let go and let God." After all, we do not heal, God does. We are simply vehicles and shells that allow It to express through us. And we must constantly remind ourselves of that, and understand that it is not "us" anymore. If not, we are playing God and not letting God be God.

Part II: How to Channel Your Thinking for Healing

We believe that time is external and carries us along, when really it is alive and conscious within itself. Synchronicity goes beyond tangibility. It is a series of events which then lead into other events. This is not something tangible in this world as you have experienced it. The embryonic state, the fluid state that I refer to as the mind of God, carries all the possibilities of what can be. It carries an electromagnetic charge as well.

We also have the ability to willfully collect this charge and utilize it. We can then control these other effects which flow from it, and so on. Some people call this Spirit, some call it by other names. I realize this force, which is not tangible, is at work at all times. I know that another person's field is flowing into my field and everything around it, all intermeshed together endlessly. This is what I use as a basis when I am working with someone's field. I automatically tune into and feel all the fields to retrieve information, which is a synchronistic flow of events in which we have participated. It's a flow of events, and we can trace any issue to its causal moment within a person's life.

Getting started: The Beginning Plan. Know what you want and see the goal in its final form

Imagine and focus on the person in front of you. Imagine them in what you perceive to be a perfect form. See the body to be harmonious, whole and perfect, working as a finely-tuned machine in perfect flow in his/her life. What you are doing is bringing in the word "imagination." You are imaging in action. You are watching this perfectly-tuned person and holding that thought, for as long as you can, the best you can, without any extraneous thoughts coming in. Even if the person is complaining of some disease or dis-ease, refuse to see that. Only see the perfection because that is what you are working with at this time. If for some reason you are unable to hold this visual, you must begin again.

After you have visualized everything in perfection, then give attention to what appears to be the physical or emotional disorder. So, first you're working on the concept of a perfect, well operating physical shell that we are, the blood and every cellular piece that brings us together in structure in an electrical matrix. Then you concentrate and see the perfection. The next step is that you see it working without the physical discomfort. Again, healing is a universal principal, a law, which takes the impressions of our thoughts and acts upon them.

Visualize the person in their perfection. Hold that image

Let's say the person you are talking to says, "I'm sick, I don't feel well...I need attention, I need a drink... I have to stay home from school." That's their sabotage.

Once you have attacked the person's thought with the image of it's perfection, your thought will bind to the other person. They will find themselves thinking along the same lines as long as you are thinking, and knowing it with surety. If you can maintain that thought, the old man or old woman upstairs (which is really inside of you) will take over from that point. That's how it is. It will take over. As long as you don't worry because worry will then be a prayer, and that will become your sabotage. Healing takes faith and trust in Self, God, It, The Nameless One, whatever name you choose. You can help eliminate another person's, or your own, false thought.

Know that it is done

Finish the treatment with your realization and your trust that it is done. Walk away, don't let another thought come in your head. If it does, you have sabotaged the effort. If this is the case, start over. That's why it is so important to learn focus, keeping that concentrated effort. That's why concentration and meditation are useful tools.

Once you have started to master these things, you will learn that you truly have the power of life and death over creation. You will get to see the manifestation not only in yourself, but in other people as well. We will begin to notice our adeptness in other aspects of non-linear and physical creation. That's how dynamic it is.

As we build the person up for perfection we are planting seeds in remembrance of what we and they already have known in life, but haven't been reminded of (re-minded-of). Bringing back the memories of the mind. Remembering. Re-membering it all together. Bringing it all back together. Of what we were originally born to be in the first place. Until now, we've taken on the difficult road of life. Following the "survival mode" technique and approach to life. Because that is what we have been taught. That's what our mothers and fathers taught us, what their fathers and mothers taught them, and so on for generations upon generations. That's hereditary. Each and every thought can carry on for generations.

Again, the law and the truth are the basis of healing. A person does not heal, the law and the truth do. We don't treat each organ of the body as individual, but we see the body to be whole and perfect, a finely tuned machine. When I first started working with healing, I would put my hands over someone's head and I would tell God to get busy because I wasn't sure what I was doing. God did take over because I trusted It to. I knew it wasn't me.

See the body as perfect. At first, when I felt unsure of what I was doing, I would say, "OK God, this person has a cold." I would envision that person I was working with in a perfect state without a cold. I imagined it melting away and the person in a perfect state. And it would be so. Once you see this completely, you then drop it like a hot potato and let go of the impression or thought. Because once you have that old thought, you will have to begin again. That's how I started thirty years ago and then it began to flow as time went on. You can start this way, too. It is a great place to start. You can learn to focus completely for just that moment. Practice this and it will develop within you.

You can create anything with your thoughts. There is no incurable disease, in my understanding, if the person you are working with will accept what you are doing, and know it is meant to be for them. Your work with them will help them immediately or over time. It will help them to be more comfortable in their life that's left if that is what is meant to be. Perhaps the disease was supposed to be part of their life because that is what their whole life has brought them to. And you can help them be more comfortable within the remaining time of their life.

When you feel the healing sensations, you are experiencing the use of the law in action. The law knows nothing about disease, it only acts. I've seen tumors disappear, I've seen thousands of people's lives change drastically.

Very few diseases are inherited, most are initiated in utero or in the birthing process. Remember the asthmatics we discussed earlier? I have learned that as children grow up, as they grow older, all their subjective reactions from events throughout their life (i.e. death, divorce, or other troubles that result in their lives) manifests on a biological and physiological level and eventually their health begins to suffer.

Events that happen in our lives, the ones we take on as part of our lives, the dramas and traumas, remain in our cellular memory. We will feel the effects of these things in ways of dis-ease or disease. Disease is actually not knowing or understanding our truer nature. Contagious disease surrounds the patient with an aura of magnetic atmosphere that can be worked with. You do not have to catch anything from anyone, unless you accept that in your life.

Part III: What Is a Morphic Field?
What Is an Aura?
What Does It Look Like?

Morphic fields carry memories of information regarding an individual's responses of any form. They are connected to the physical body, though not separate, and can be located within and around the area of an individual. Everything of your existence is in the morphic fields. Many "New Agers" refer to this as an external aura.

There is no separation with the field though it can be discussed regarding various topics. Just as the arm is separate from the leg and can be discussed individually, it is still part of the same physical organism with a similar makeup.

You can see light around all things. This light reflects the vibratory rate and the life consciousness that object carries. This can be distinguished even further. If the ability to see this light is developed, you will be able to see that certain objects have different vibratory rates. This "sight" will develop with experience.

Many people are able to see or sense colors around other people. This is an indicator of another consciousness that allows us to work with healing. When a trauma is released through healing, it can sometimes be seen as waves coming off a person's body much like heat waves off a highway on a hot day. Some people see the release as smoke, some smell it, and others see it as wisps coming off the body. Sometimes people see the healing through a person's tears. It is easier to see this energy with peripheral vision. Just *gaze* about six inches above someone's head and beyond and then let your peripheral vision take over. Practice this and then it will become automatic. You can also accomplish this by staring at someone's forehead and then tune into your peripheral vision and let it wander into the space beyond the body.

Some people see colors around other people's heads. If you see a reddish or pinkish glow, this indicates a headache. If you see gray, stick with it until it takes its form as a color. There is a color around the periphery of each person. If you see globules following someone, they are thinking very intently. If you see a pink glow away from the head, then the headache happened several days ago. The further away from the body, the greater length of time has passed since the headache or injury. Remember, not everyone sees colors, each of us has our own unique way of perceiving. By practicing, you will learn about your own unique ability. The morphic fields may show you color. They also may show you the "disease body."

What is a disease-body? What does it look like?

Disease-body is the spiritual, biological and physical manifestation of "dis-ease," and is carried in the memory. It is basically composed of ammonia and methane gas, which is deteriorative in action. This is the disturbance you feel, see or smell. That's what I feel, that's what you will sense, too. It's a combustion process within the cellular process that you are actually feeling the effects of before and after physical manifestation. You may be able to see this gaseous body. It can look grayish in color, or a distorted, dingy yellow at times. It could be other colors, but they will seem very dingy and muddy-looking. You can sometimes feel it as a pressure, or a weight, or an electrical discharge, or tingling, which is the consciousness of light deteriorating the disease. It will sometimes feel like a void, or it will feel dirty or sticky. If you can get yourself out of the way, your hands will feel it. Use the surface of the skin on your palms to "feel" it.

Some people can smell disease. Each disease has its own odor. Arthritis smells like burning rubber. Cancer smells very, sickly sweet. Each person perceives disease uniquely. As you practice with healing, you will become more familiar with the differences in the way you experience other people's disease bodies.

For every person who has something out of synch in their fields, there is directly related symptom of something that they feel is out of kilter physically, biologically or emotionally. Every dysfunctional dynamic a person experiences in their life, that is not attended to, will eventually become manifested on a biological and physical level. Emotional distress will most certainly develop into physical/biological distress, and you can feel this in a person's fields. When feeling someone's field, therefore, you are feeling their current state of being, their history and the life that will be.

Remember, it's only energy. You are not getting "cooties." You can't. Another simple truth is this: **"No darkness, no shadow can stand in the light."** It's simply another form of energy.

Trust that what you sense in another person is correct

When you begin to learn healing, you usually start by learning to feel the disease body. This will provide you with the "proofs" you need to know that this is real for you. Then you have to accept what you perceive and trust what you are imagining to be true. Once you trust yourself when you are standing before someone, in the light, then you will see more and more clearly your ability to heal others. Once you have been practicing with feeling the disease body, you will become more acutely tuned into the different feelings of each and every disease. You will see that these images may occur for just a flash of a second, you will learn to tune in. You will learn what to watch for. Remember, you are only feeling the cellular memory from distress experienced during a person's life.

Arthritis is the lack of motion and flexibility within the joints. This stems from the inability to grasp issues due to a stubborn understanding. If you crack your knuckles, this will disrupt the sinovial fluid in the joints, and it will not properly flow. When this happens, you get stiffness and the inability to grasp. This happens on an emotional level as well.

Again, asthma is a form of panic disorder usually resulting from a childhood experience or birth. It is a pattern that has taken on a physical manifestation from a childhood causal moment. To find out when it started, listen to your intuition, and plant a seed as far as determining when this disorder first started within them. Then work on it. Wait until you feel something happen in their body. Concentrate on looking past them and you will somehow sense when it all began. You will get a sense based on your way of perceiving.

Concentrated focus

Concentrated focus is the key to reaching your goal. The intense ability to focus and keep that focus and concentration is the actual dimensional basis of experience of other dimensional mindfulness. We have the ability to control the power of life and death over creation.

An example of what focus can accomplish

Many years ago, I was fortunate to be able to watch a woman work with a child. I did not know the child would be there. The child arrived with a broken arm. This woman began to work with the child. She held this little broken arm on her lap. She was working with what she described as magnetic forces. Within several minutes, the broken bone actually moved from the broken to the natural position. This woman used electromagnetic healing, a very strong and powerful tool for the person who develops that aspect of healing. Just as Uri Geller works with the electrical, magnetic composition to actually change the molecular structure in order to bend spoons. He works with focused concentration.

Another healing experience

A man came to see me who had been diagnosed with a nerve disease that left him in extreme pain. The nerves were in a constant state of deterioration and he could no longer walk because of the intense pain on the bottom of his feet. He was diagnosed when he was ten years old and was told there was no cure. He came to me as a forty year old man, wearing special braces for his legs which helped ease the discomfort. The pain in his calf muscles was not as intense as it had been since he had the braces made, which gave him good physical support. I worked on him to see how I could help. The next day, he called me and was practically yelling on the phone, "You're not going to believe this! My calf muscle is bigger and I don't need the braces anymore! My feet don't hurt anymore!" This pain originated for him almost thirty years prior to my visit with him. And it had been growing since then and made him who he was until that day. Healing helps these causal memories to melt away and to change someone's life.

This has been validated for me thousands of times during healing sessions. I am awed by the gift that all of us have to offer one another, if we can simply tune in and understand that it is available to each and every one of us.

It is important to understand that people are affected by healing in their own way. In some way or other the person will be affected, but in the parameters of their speed, in their time, in the course of what is to be in their life. It is not up to us to decide just how a person is affected from our healing. It is up to God. We do not know how others or we are going to be affected. The outcome, how it affects the person's life, is not to be determined by us. There are so many facets of a person's life that is affected from even one causal moment, that we do not know how things will progress. Our only resort is to trust.

It is also important to know that healing does not, and can not, harm another. You can do only good with Healing. Trust this. Know this.

Part IV: Scanning the Morphic Fields

Review: The Palm-to-Palm Exercise
What the sensation is to experience sensing another's energy

Stand up and face your partner. Make sure you are in a quiet environment so you can focus more easily. Place your hands in the "pat-a-cake" position. Bend your elbows at a 90-degree angle and turn your hands so one of your palms is facing the ceiling, the other facing the floor. Put the left palm up and the right palm down. Have your partner do the same so that your palms face one another's. Your palms should not be touching. Hold your palms one inch to one and a half inches away from your partner. Do not make physical contact.

Close your eyes. Begin to feel the energy between your hands. Feel it on your palms. That's the energy that's within you that is waiting and begging for you to give. It's so real, it's dynamic. It is the life force that is flowing between you. That's the flow of energy. Slowly start to move up and down a little bit. Feel this on the skin of your hands. Move slowly. Continue to move your hands slowly up and down a little. Feel the attraction and the pull of the energy. It will feel like a pressure inside. You will feel something between your hands. Experience the inner and outer limits of the electrical matrix of body. Feel how great it is. How tall it is. Move your hands apart until you barely feel it and open your eyes to see how far apart your hands are.

You are feeling the electrical matrix we are all composed of and the extrusion of the spiritual body. While you are doing this, if you feel something in a special place in your body, for example, your wrist, that is because you are un-log jamming something. The flow of energy is giving life, it is clearing the log jam which is in that spot.

This exercise is the same as when you work with someone in scanning. There is no difference, this is the exact same feeling, same property.

Part V: Using Scanning for Healing: How to Scan, What You Will Sense

Initial Scanning Position

Your partner stands in front of you with their arms at their side. Meanwhile, you will begin the process of scanning: Position your hands over the top of your partner's head without touching them. There is no need for direct contact. Wait until you feel that same sensory body that you just felt with the Palm-to-Palm exercise. Your eyes can be open or closed, God doesn't care, go with whichever way you are more comfortable. At this time, your partner may also feel something, or they may not.

Concentrated focus is imperative to scanning. Realize what is to be your unique ability

Tune in and feel that part of the body that is extruding outside of you. You do not need to touch the other person, keep your hands away from their body. Move your hands around a little, keeping them side by side or splitting them apart. See which technique works best for you to continue sensing your partner's energy.

With your hands, travel slowly down the body, along the neck, the shoulders, each arm and work your way down to the waist area. Move slowly and you will feel, at some place, a little distortion in the field. It could be feel like a void. Or it could feel like a sensation of a different kind, such as heat, cold, or static. This is a stopping area. Wait there until that feeling goes away. You will feel a flow, or the other person will feel a flow.

Tune into what your unique perception of knowing is. Have your partner tune in to their unique perception as well. Tell each other what you feel and when you feel it. Tell each other when you notice some kind of change. Wait until the pulsing breaks if you are feeling the pulse of the body. The body has about 16 pulses per minute in its true health or form, in the flow of the heat cycle.

Go with the flow. Trust it

Now wait until the pulsing (or whatever you feel) dissipates, goes away, or flows. And then go to the next area. Keep moving down the body until you get to the waist. Then wait there. You have to move slowly. If you get some flash of information, whether you hear it, see it, or feel it, do not negate this, accept this. Trust this. Do not edit what you receive, speak plainly and honestly. Ask your partner if they remember something regarding this spot. Something happened in their life that is being reflected in each spot where you feel the distortion or difference. Something has happened. At one time, they had an injury or an ache or pain in that spot. They are carrying a memory of that in their cells. It could have been a long time ago.

Be Sensitive to any changes in temperature, open spaces, sensations

Be sensitive to any temperature changes, open spaces or different kinds of sensations in different areas. You may feel electricity.

Anxiety and worry is generally located around the shoulders and neck, sometimes in the gut. Every person carries it in a unique way.

When you feel something farther away from the body, it is a thing of the past. This is the drama and trauma of something that happened a long time ago but it is still affecting them. You can work at this extraneous place. They may or may not feel it, but this will help to change the current dynamics of the causal time-period of their life.

Even if you take your hands down when you are working with a person, when you raise your hands again you will feel where you left off. However, you may find that some part of it has dissipated.

Then... wait until you feel a flow

You are waiting until you feel the flow. When you feel it, then they are becoming more healed within themselves. This is what initiates true regeneration. What you are doing in a quantum scientific dynamic is working at a molecular level. In this case, it is working with the "spiritual molecule." You are giving it life in a different perspective. You are helping it to remember, to remind itself of its perfection. Self, God, whatever you call It, is doing the actual healing instead of us doing it. You will feel your indicators. It might be difficult to perceive that, but it will come. You don't have to provide anything except intent. That's why focus is important. Remember, God will not hurt you or anyone else. We are the ones who hurt ourselves, and carry the pain and go through the emotional dramas and traumas.

You started doing this not knowing what you would be doing or feeling. Intent took over for you; it has a consciousness and an intelligence. It knows what to do with or without us. We're just there as a vehicle. For it to utilize us.

In the future, the person being scanned may need more of this interaction or they may just need this one experience to have a seed planted and they can take over for themselves. You will know.

Part VI: Scanning and Timelines: Working with Scanning on the Lower Body

When you are finished working on the upper body, then begin on the lower body. You will start at the waist and move down. Once you reach the hips, begin to work with one leg at a time.

As a reference, there are age associations to go along with various segments one's legs. If you feel a void or a change in an adult's field, it corresponds to the following ages:

The waist relates to the age on or near 21, depending on the person's structure
The hip bone relates to the age on or near 15
The knee relates to the age on or near 10
The ankle relates to the age on or near 2
The foot relates to the first year of life (Note: I teach this extensively in the seminars.)

When you feel something in between these areas (for example, between the hip and waist would be between the ages of 15 and 21) you can focus on that age range and get information about what happened, and at what age. With practice, you will sense things much more quickly. This topic merits a book of its own.

Part VII: Healing Happens in Scanning

Accept it as done, do not doubt it. As soon as you doubt, you will blow the whole prayer. This doubt will only serve as sabotage of your intent. Healing will only happen when you get out of the way. Just try this, even though you do not know what would normally happen. All you have to do is trust, and it is done. Do not look over your shoulder and doubt. That is totally unnecessary. Understanding of intent and knowing is an art in itself.

While scanning, try to get a sense inside of what is wrong in those spots of distortion. Be sensitive to yourself. Use the same intent to sense, see, feel or hear an impression, when you hit a spot, of what might be a disturbance. Ask the person if this is so or associated with their dilemma in any way.

Feel the distress, but not in you and not on them. Concentrate. When you feel a little area, let your Self tell you what might not be correct in that person's life. Ask them if that is true. Get an impression in some way. Concentrate on what you are sensing: hearing, feeling, seeing, knowing, whatever your sensation is. Pay attention. This represents how you perceive energy and its dynamical changes.

Part VIII: Frequently Asked Questions about Scanning and Healing

Q: **What if you want to work on someone who does not believe in Healing? They think it is all bunk, hocus-pocus nonsense. Can they still gain the effects of healing?**

A: It is not wrong to do good. You can provide helpful benefits of healing to anyone, as long as it is your intent to do such a thing. I know many people who have helped others while they are asleep. Your intent is the key to helping others. Remember though, you do not decide what needs to be healed, God does. You must trust this. You don't need permission from people to help them do better.

Q: **But then, doesn't that go against the thing where, if you are trying to heal them, maybe it's not the thing for them, at that time, to be healed. Remember you said we all need to be at certain places at certain times.**

A: Yes. Because we are leaving it up to God and maybe it is our prayer that is needed for not only their growth, but our own growth as well. But I will not work with someone who doesn't want me to work on them, nor will I work on someone for something they were forced by another to be in front of me. Nor will I work with anyone who just wants to test me to see if I can find something. When someone approaches us, it must be for help. At times I have told some people to leave. Maybe that person was brought in front of us with something not being right in their life, but in actuality they were sent before us because we had to accomplish some form of growth and they are the chosen catalyst. This is our factor of growth that is needed, to be able to give ourselves in one way or another. Maybe it is not our place. We never know. It's just like saying how do you know there isn't an angel coming up to you on the street dressed in skin as a person? Who are we to judge?

Q: **Do you feel energy moving through you all the time that you are working on someone?**

A: I do. They do not always feel what I feel. You may feel heat. I feel a particular vibrational pattern. I've learned how to relate to it as heat, cold, static, and other sensations. Other people may feel cold, but I associate another vibrational pattern with cold. I may know that an emotional catharsis is coming on, and that's OK too. Or I may know there is a constriction in the emotional catharsis and I'll break or release that constriction. I'll feel the vibrational pattern of "stuckness." Not so stuck that you are dying, but that you have stuff in you that is not totally flowing. That's the way I feel it. Then, I know it is done when I feel the flow through my body. That is one of my indicators. You may have a similar or different indicator. There are times when I do not know precisely what I am sensing at first. I have to wait for the information like anyone else, though mostly it is immediate.

Q: Most of the time when I am doing the healing of people, they feel the warmth or whatever. This one person said they felt so cold and shivered. It made me nervous.

A: That was their experience of it.

Q: But they still experienced a healing?

A: Yes, definitely. As soon as you start saying "I'm nervous about it," that is your sabotage because you are pulling back a little bit.

Q: Well, it scared me a little bit. I thought why is she feeling cold? She said it so fearfully...

A: God does not hurt. We hurt ourselves.

Q: Can you work on a child when he/she is sleeping?

A: Yes. One way of working on a little child who is sick or unwell or has something that is not right with them in their life is while they are sleeping. We can put our hands above them, without touching, and scan their entire body and we can wait until we feel a flow of life force, pulsing between this hand and the other hand. When we can get to approximately 16 pulsations a minute, we know the body is in flow and their situation is taken care of. That's the power of life and death over creation in that respect.

Q: **How do you help someone who has chronic pain or discomfort? What do you mean when you say you can help them embrace the pain?**

A: A sufferer might be creating the pain to fulfill its reality, but then the pain turns into something beyond their experience and intent of what they took on in life. One can get beyond the suffering of it to a place where they no longer need to suffer. When you are embracing the pain, you are taking the conscious or sub-consciousness of it and embracing it so it is no longer an interference in your life cycle. Because you are not fighting it anymore, you are not suppressing it anymore. Does that ring a bell?

Q: **When you say to imagine the perfection of "it" are you talking about the perfection of the destructive pattern? Or the perfection that you are imposing?**

A: In this discussion, I'm referring to the perfection I am imposing. And I am going in and working with the perfection of the destructive pattern. When someone says, "I'll pray for you" because you are going through a rough time, I say. "Don't bother." Because when someone prays for you, they do not know the full dynamic that you are going through and what the outcome is that is needed for you. They cannot actually pray for you unless they are a Master Teacher or some kind of great, insightful person who knows exactly what the situation should be for you.

When someone is praying for you they are giving you energy. To do what? Stay chaotic? Energy is a great influx of stuff, but it has to be directed or there is more chaos. If you don't have the focal point for your direction yet, what is someone else going to do for you? I'm a person that tries to live my life by my word. So everything has to be real for me. So if I don't have my thoughts or intent together yet, I don't want to send someone energy. If someone wants to pray to God for me, fine. Or if they know a specific element of that pattern that I need prayer for and I know they will do it, I say fine. Otherwise, most people say they are going to pray but then go about their business, they don't really pray for you at all.

Q: **Will we feel the same sense of healing with every person?**

A: It's not going to be the same with every person. It will always be different. When working with someone, you may come to a log jam. Nothing is ever completely blocked or there would be no life. There will always be a trickle. If we can stay there for a moment until we feel the flow of it, then the life force is opening it up for them. Then we move on. The log jam is a representation of various emotional dramas and traumas of our lives which affect us physiologically. By providing the life force a chance to break through, we are taking care of that situation right there. Not only is it enough to break through, but you may very well be saving a person's life. The person has free will to accept within themselves any part or all of that what you are doing, but it is not a conscious decision.

Q: **Well, I don't think I have proved to myself that I can do this. I still have this question about whether what I see around people is accurate and what I feel with my hands is really more than just sensation of my hands.**

A: I understand. The only way that you will see that you have proved it to yourself is if you try it with someone else, do it again, and have that so-called proof again. You may doubt that and then try it on someone else. You may need to repeat your experiences again and again. Then you will doubt that. Do this again and again and again, doubting it each and every time. That doubt is the mass mind in action telling you this can't be happening. This is our immediate intellectual response. That's what we're trained to do in this world. Believe me, I have been in your place. I have learned finally to stop thinking, "OK, if this is really real, I'm going to try it again and I expect to get the same results as last time. And if it's true, I will accept it a little bit more, not too much, not all of it at once, but a little at a time." I won't believe it until I see it many, many more times in the future. Once I see an effect, a difference, either immediately or within 24 hours, then I will accept a little bit more and try again. Just a little bit at a time. Keep at it. You will see for yourself that this is a reality.

You are smart to doubt what you are doing. It is more "real" to do what you are doing. Feel how you are feeling when you doubt it. I know because I doubted, too. I wanted to see the proof in the pudding. I wanted to see the whole hog in front of me. I don't want to believe anything anyone tells me until I know it's true. If I keep trying it and it keeps working, there must be something there telling me that something here may be real. It will keep happening again and again.

I challenge you to keep doubting. I think it's good to do that. I must do that, too, and now I have learned through experience, and I am still learning through doubt. But I wouldn't have learned what I know now unless I had the experience before. Got it? I have to be real in this world. And I admire you for that because that shows a sense of integrity.

Q: **When my partner worked on me, I had my eyes closed. I felt heat in the cavities of my face when his hands were near my face. I didn't feel any change in it, and when I opened my eyes he was working in another area, but I still felt the heat in my face. Why?**

A: This is because the healing was still working. It's what I refer to as "fire fighting fire." A greater consciousness is left inside somewhere in the body to do the work. We don't need to do anything. We are letting It take over from there. I'll bet that he was working on your abdominal area. The abdomen always relates to the head and vice versa.

Q: I came to see you about six weeks ago about not eating lots of fatty things, and you worked on this for me. Ever since then, I noticed there's a part of my brain that still sees it there and says, "Oh yes, eat that." Then I'll take a bite or two and get nauseous, and put it down. It's been great. I can drive by Colonel Sanders now so easily.

A: Hooray! That is because I was able to work with the causal moment that created this craving in you. You must have been ready to let it go. I just provided the catalyst to help you. The tool I use is what I call phasing.

Q: Is psychological disease the same as physiological? Does it feel the same?

A: Yes. I feel it the same and I work with it in a different way. But yes, it is the same in body/mind reference.

Q: Can you clarify the various stages which take you from a causal moment up to the state where physical and biological disease occurs?

A: First we experience a mental perception regarding a thought or event. This perception generally stems from the causal moment or moments when we first experienced the event and the conversations of what we've been taught all our lives. This original thought becomes your living prayer and from that moment on it will manifest itself in you in one way or another at one time or another. What we feel and what we think is what we teach our children to be. They will become of a similar nature in pattern and idea.

Next comes the enactment of the emotional response, the hurt, the fear, the pain, the anxiety, the sadness, the distress of whatever it is. Even if it pertains to feeling that for someone else. When you feel the hurt, despair, sadness, pain or anxiety for yourself or someone else, you have just planted a seed inside yourself.

After you have the emotional onset of it all, it turns into a biological factor. This can happen right away or it will be manifested later in life.

The biological reaction occurs during the amount of time it takes to finally build up to that place. Then you have the physiological onset and it is manifested in the form of an illness.

If you know It in yourself, you will realize you no longer have to be chained to the past anymore. If you know it. Realize you no longer have to be chained to the past. The past is past. Let go of it. You are not there anymore.

Q: **How can I get rid of my own headache?**

A: If you have a headache or you feel one coming on, try the following: You will know when to do it. It's when you hear yourself think or even say out loud, "Oh no, I feel this headache coming on." At this moment you can catch yourself in your thought and say, "Wait. If I can realize that the headache is coming on then I can also realize and imagine (image in action) something else too. I'm going to do something here. I'm going to step out of myself and see the headache as a stream and let it go right on by me. I'm going to stop and think that when I step back I will not let the stream hit me." You will realize that you didn't have a headache for that moment or two. Now, try it again. Step back again. For a moment you didn't have that headache again.

Now we can take this one step further and say, "OK, I see you. I feel you. I sense you. But you are going to have to wait a moment, I have something else to do. Wait here and I will be right back." Then ditch it. Walk away quickly, think of something else to get your mind off of it. Watch what happens, you will not have that headache for a longer time. You will soon realize that you can set a pattern where you won't have to ever take on a headache, or discomfort or pain.

We have the power of life and death over creation. If we just practice it, it becomes real in our life just as easily as the other stuff in our life becomes real. These are all tools for us. As a matter of fact, it was more difficult to get out of synch in life that it was to stay real, or in synch.

Q: **If you feel someone else's pain, it then becomes your own prayer. How can you reverse that? I can't imagine seeing someone in pain and not in some way feeling sorry for them. I thought empathy is good. Isn't it?**

A: This is where we have to differentiate, this is where we have to step out of ourselves, this is where we have to separate ourselves and let go and let God. Say, "OK God, you are using me inside to work on this person. I don't want to take any of this stuff on. I don't want to leave here with whatever they have. So, you go ahead and do it." Accept that something else is happening through you. If you can do that, in separating yourself, just that trust, you won't take on anything. You need not take it personally, you are not the savior, God is, and that is the difference.

Q: **I'm not clear about the difference between praying for people and the fact that it's not our place to know what's right for someone else.**

A: If it's for a specific purpose for that person's life to be in less discomfort or disease, there is no wrong in offering prayer. It has to be specific though. If you know that person is hurting and you feel bad enough for that person that you don't want them to suffer anymore and you can help them wake up feeling better the next morning, that's not wrong.

Q: **So, it doesn't matter whether you do accomplish the task through healing or through prayer.**

A: Correct. It's all the same. But when someone says, "Oh, let me send you some energy." I say, "For what purpose? To make me feel better or to make me finish my tasks and still feel bad, or to help me make it through just this day?" It will be more effective if one has a focal point to focus that prayer into something constructive. If they have something they are complaining about, apply it to that. Otherwise, the prayer gets scattered.

Q: **What if you pray for the highest good for someone?**

A: What is the highest good? When you pray to God for a person and you don't know what to do, then you could pray that they be taken care of in the highest good or right action. When we want them to be taken care of in our way, then we are laying our stuff on them instead of God's way.

Q: **Is it possible in a day or two a person could sabotage the work you just did because of her doubting?**

A: Everyone can impose sabotage on themselves at any time. The interesting thing is that once someone has experienced healing, a seed has been planted. Anything other than the healing is going to feel uncomfortable. It's like going to a closet and finding a sweater that you used to really like. You realize that it no longer fits the same, maybe it's uncomfortable to wear and you don't like it anymore. When you try to pick up a pattern where we left it off, we find that we no longer have that other pattern so it feels uncomfortable. You will find a greater pattern taking its place naturally.

Q: **I tend to worry about so many things. How can I help myself so I don't worry so much anymore? My mom has also always been a worrier, how can I avoid being the same way?**

A: You learned how to worry from your mother. Now you are doing the same thing. You come by it honestly, but you can break this habit. You can break the mold of the conversation you grew up with all your life. You know this is not necessary anymore. You can make a choice to correct that thinking consciously. It is only a conversation!

Q: **I'm the same way that mom is, an extreme worrier. My mom was the same way while I was growing up and still is. I have two girls now and I'm always thinking, what about all those thoughts I had before. Is there a possibility of harm?**

A: Yes, it is affecting their life. And you have determined what they are going to learn to be when they grow up. The same way you are. If you keep on going this way, you will definitely lead them to be the same way you are. Generally, a guy will hold everything in and have ulcers. Someday he can say, "Thanks Mom/Dad." Why concern yourself about your children when they belong to God in the first place? Your only obligation is to house them, clothe them, feed them, and love them. The rest is up to God. All we have to learn to do is to trust God.

Q: **Why is it so hard to trust? Easy to say, easy in theory, but so hard to practice.**

A: Because we haven't been brought up to trust. No one has told us that we can. No one has reinforced it in our lives and told us that we can.

Q: **Is it possible to lose your abilities? What if you don't practice healing, will you lose the ability to heal?**

A: No. It's nothing like that. In 1972, I didn't have anything to compare this experience to. I didn't have the vast quantity of New Age believers to relate to. There were times, in the first few years of my experience, when I thought, "Oh my God, I'm losing my power!" I have since learned that you never lose anything, you simply put it aside. Nothing in life is ever lost. It is put aside and lays idle to develop into something greater later. Your experiences turn it into wisdom and you will find it's time to go on.

There may be a time when you feel you are not experiencing the healing when you are working on others. There are times I have gone to the Healing

Circle and worked with many people in healing, yet I felt that nothing was happening. Nothing. Meanwhile, there will be people saying, "That is the most powerful healing circle you have ever done!" And people will return the next time with a lack of disease, and tell me what a powerful experience they had. I had been taken out of the way, just as you will be taken out of the way in order to do it. It will be done without your participation. Then you may find you will be able to get back into it with a new, different perspective.

Q: **I have a sister-in-law who is pregnant with twins. She has been told that there is something wrong with the twins. Last year she had a baby that died. How can I help her?**

A: Visualize the outcome of perfection. Let God take over and let God do what needs be done. Not what we want to do, but what God does. Visualize the perfection and say, "OK God, here is the perfection from my sight. Let's see what you come up with." We don't know what the child coming in needs to go through nor what your sister needs to go through for experience that's going to affect the world around her. They might have something to learn too. We don't know where people are going to come into play. In a situation like this, because this situation affects a lot of people, we have to visualize our idea of perfection and then hand it over to God and see what happens. We're pretty amazed, usually, from what happens with our simple prayer of interjection.

Q: **If you are working on someone and you work through some of the blockages that they have, will you always have to work on every area?**

A: No because the more experienced you become, the more attuned you become to the memory of it. It may be so subtle, and away from the body that shows that the experience was a long time ago. It may be so subtle and so uninfluential in his/her life. The person is doing well in life without having to work on it.

Q: **Do you work with animals the same way you work with people?**

A: Yes.

Creator

Chapter 8

Trust & Love

Creator

"You have choice in every moment. If you don't like the way things are, choose again, choose differently."

Creator

Part I: Fear No More

What Is Fear? Why Does It Have So Much Power over Us?

Fear is our negator in this world. It grabs us and says, "Please don't trust because if you do, I will lose you." Fear has a consciousness that wants to keep you away from the Divinity Within. It is very afraid, that's why we call it fear.

We can't really be afraid of fear because it is only doing what it knows to do. We can picture fear as an entity that comes in and says, "Give me life." It says, "Please don't love yourself. Remember those bad things from your past? Well, that shows you can't love yourself. So you should be afraid and stick with me."

Fear discounts everything and anything of a constructive, beneficial or inspirational nature. You can't hate it because it doesn't have free will like we have. It only knows how to do one thing, to distract us and take us away from the trust in our divinity. We can do one of several things: we can ignore it, listen to fear and continue on in life. Or we can trust that we have a choice to do otherwise, to grow and learn. We need fear in order to balance our life. We need it so we can recognize it and then decide which way we want to proceed. Everything that doesn't inspire us, or lift us up, is based on fear. I call this the "conversation" of the "mass mind."

Fear is a separation that we have created as man and woman have gotten far away from the Creator of their life's existence. We have gotten so far away that we begin to look for something greater outside of ourselves. In reality this greater aspect outside of us doesn't exist at all. We have been taught to look for everything outside of ourselves. We can look for it for the rest of our lives, but will never find it. In turn, this develops into philosophy and questions of what is "out there" that is greater than us.

It's not outside; the Divinity is inside us, always has been, and will always be within. It is not separate from us; we are all a part of it. It is simple to say, yet often difficult to comprehend because we have not been taught this perspective. We have been taught the perspective of separateness from something greater, that there are fears and consequences to our actions.

You are not separate from God, because God is within you, within each of us. Everything else is conversation of the mass mind, trying to keep you within its grasp so you will see and believe exactly as they do.

We can train ourselves to pay attention to our thoughts and feelings, each and every inspirational or negating thought, and then make a decision which to keep and which to let go. Once you are conscious of your thoughts, you can train yourself to let go of any negating thoughts. Try it for a few days. Count the number of negating thoughts you have in one day. Do it for several more days and watch how they diminish in number. It takes concentration and practice. You can do this to help reduce those things that have become fearful and negating in your life.

What is sabotage?

Sabotage is that which creates doubt in the "OK-ness" of our lives. It is what we do to eliminate the trust we can have in knowing that "everything really is OK." We have a tendency not to see this because of our tainted vision of life. We tend to sabotage ourselves at every opportunity available. This is completely unnecessary.

All these sabotages extend from our childhood experiences. Every single one of them. You can blame them on "past life experiences," or anything else. If you do, then you know it is a carry over from the previous life and possibly the ones before that. What difference does it make? As long as you address it now, what difference does it make where it came from or when? The fact is it will still register in your morphic field of today and can be worked with in this life.

You can choose to create your own change at every moment

Why not go ahead and work it out now? If you can just recognize that there was some event that helped lead you to feel how you feel today, even if you don't remember exactly how it started, you can choose to work it out differently.

It takes a simple recognition to understand that there was something which helped you feel about things the way you do, and led you to become the "who you are," and "what you are" now. There were causal events in your life that built you to be the person you are today. There is no need to carry it on. We have a choice, free will, to choose to change or sustain anything at any given moment in our life.

You choose your place in the world. You decide what you wish to sustain and what you wish to change in your world

The world around you, your friends and the living environment around you are the very things that encourage you to stay as you are. They encourage you not to choose a different way of looking at anything. They, too, can be your sabotage, and could be the things that, up until now, you believed keep you "secure" in that world. If you can let it go, and let in the Divinity within, you will find yourself not always reacting to the world around you, but instead choosing your place within the world.

Part II: We All Need "Down Time."

Down Times Are Meant to Happen

Down times are given to us on a golden platter specifically in order to force us to take a break. It is a time for you to learn and grow in some aspect of your life.

This may last five minutes, a day, a week, or persist over several months. I've had periods last up to three months. During that time I thought I lost everything in my life, that I had served my purpose and nothing more was going to be happening in my life. Then I realized this wasn't so. I knew this when a woman approached me to work on her. I thought everything was gone and nothing would happen. I was wrong. That became one of the most powerful healing experiences in my life. It was my proof. I learned to trust in my down times. You could trust yours as well.

When you are feeling ill

We know that when we are ill our body is actually performing a cleansing. Then, why can't you get the benefits of the cleansing without being sick? You can.

What I do is that I imagine a stream of consciousness coming into my head helping me to realize I should be feeling bad with a cold, or the flu, or whatever. Then I step back and imagine that stream passing right by me. This is when I realize that I don't have that bad feeling anymore. That is until I start thinking about it again and it finds me again. Then I do the same thing in my mind again and again until I fully let go of the expectation of feeling poorly.

For example, I'll imagine a cold, and say to it, "No. Wait here, I'll be right back. You can come in me and go ahead, move in and put up your pictures, light your fire, put up your tent... you can do all the things you want to do. But, I'll be right back. You wait here. I can't accept you right now because I have something else to do." Then walk away from it. Try this.

Don't you remember all the times when you have thought, "Oh! I'm starting to feel sick, but I can't get sick right now because I have so much going on, or I have to do this really important thing." And you don't get sick at that time! But the minute the thing you were working on is gone, BAM! You get sick. In the back of your mind, that was your original prayer.

This is because you accepted it into your system at that moment; you let it in and invited it to stay with you. You were the one who put the illness on hold. You can continue to do this indefinitely if you choose to.

This broadens in concept. You still need your down time in order to be cleansed and grow. You do not need to have the illness ordinarily associated with it at these times to accomplish this goal. In fact, you are going through cleansings all the time. It is just that we resort to feeling ill in order to allow ourselves to take the time to physically regroup. Our conversations that we need to be sick, to have a break in life, constantly reinforce themselves.

Give yourself permission to take voluntary down times. Time to meditate, sleep, relax, read a book. You don't have to get sick in order to have down time. You know where we all learned that, right? Consider this discussion carefully and see how it relates to your life.

Developing confidence and assurance in healing. Take time to practice

You will develop skill and expertise with time and practice. All the techniques we presented are tools to aid in your development. The more you adapt, the more adept you will become at handling your tools.

The more you practice, the more confident you will become. You will find your specialties as you are shown what your specialties are. They will become a more conscious part of you. Every person has abilities to varying degrees. Everyone is unique.

Be bold and step out into what you have learned. Few people on earth have recognized themselves within this philosophy and reality of this kind of healing. You have learned to call on the Divinity within your Self, without getting bogged down or sabotaged in the process.

The constant flow of giving

Healing initiates regeneration by approaching the causes of dilemmas, the mass mind that negates the healing of others and ourselves. We heal others as we heal ourselves. Whatever we see in others is mirrored in our own lives and we must recognize this. Only then can we work on the other person as we are in the process of recognition.

Our purpose is to edify something greater within our own Self. God is the ecosystem of all creation. It is composed of unlimited existences of our existence, as we are in God. It is unceasing and continually unfolding, constantly in flow. It is not static, not frozen so that we can say it is separate from us. It is within us and it only knows a flow of giving, constantly giving and finding Its level within us as we allow it to happen. It is good and it is within.

Whatever we accept is what we get

We can do anything we want with it; we can use it for destruction, if we choose, and then we will live with the law of cause and effect for those uses. We can use it to improve and manifest even greater that which we know and then we will live within the law of cause and effect for that too. Whatever world we want is the one we get.

Everything in life is your stepping-stone. Everything is there for your growth and development. As long as you realize these things are just tools, we can not hurt people. If you do something in innocence, the other person will be taken care of. If you do something purposefully and with ignorance, then the repercussions always follow. This too is of the law of cause and effect. Be aware of this.

If you go into healing with the intent of not hurting anyone else, the situation will be taken care of for you. It is done. You will be taken care of.

Our purpose is to be more conscious of that small still Voice within, which then leads us to be more empowered in our lives. As we do this, we are letting It live more externally, more consciously in our life.

The greatest attribute is love

The basis for everything is love. Loving ourselves is the most important aspect of any form of healing. Love is creative and protective. Being objective is an opportunity that gives us a chance to love and be loved. It is a softening of a heart. Many of us have a resistance to that. We now are given the opportunity to love ourselves.

There is something within us that is begging us to honor it, to acknowledge it. This thing inside, called Self, is alive and well. We are just shells for it. Self is with us at every moment of our lives, talking to us, guiding us and directing us in order for us to listen to it.

When we try not to follow the way of the rest of the world, the mass mind will pounce on us in order to get us back to its way of living. It will throw lots of dramas and traumas at us, especially as we move further into a spiritual life. You will become worried again. You will think, "Well that spiritual world was nice for a time, but now I have to get back to the 'real' world." Then you will get out of it and turn back to the "old" world way.

As you practice the trust that everything's OK, you can realize that God is more powerful than anything or anyone else, and you will be able to spiritually and physically survive in this brave new world that many are delving into. You will be able to create a balance between what you now know as spiritually true and co-exist with the "real" world at the same time.

The more you practice this, the easier it becomes and you will find that you can do it, but only if you trust that everything is OK. Accept this trust as you have accepted all that you have known to be true, is true. Don't let the doubts slip in. Once you fall prey to them, they will be fulfilled once again.

Now is the time to start trusting. It took your whole life to get you to this point. And now you are here to work it out.

There is no longer a need to have trust only in man

I hope that your understanding of what you refer to as God, or Self, is alive and well within you. **Creator** is here to show and reinforce this within you. We truly carry a piece of this Godliness within us and Its fulfillment is waiting only for you.

God bless you, my friend.

Addendum I

Quick Reference Guide to *Creator*

Meditations

Addendum

I. Breath of God: A breathing exercise for meditation

Read this exercise in its entirety before beginning. Study the text and what you are looking for as a result of focused breathing. Place a pad of paper and a pen or pencil nearby or on your lap. Once you have done the above, you may begin.

Imagine yourself breathing in the breath of God. Breathe it all the way in, through your sinus cavities and throughout your skull. Breathe the breath of God in through your nostrils, all the way in, and begin to feel the tingling aliveness of your nerve endings, of everything within you. Feel the alertness, the excitement in your body. Notice how the bones of your head feel. The light that you are sensing is actually becoming clearer. If you feel it in your skull, you are not really feeling it in your actual bones, but in the layer of tissue on the surface of your bones that have the nerve endings. This is merely the place where you feel the sensations.

Keep your eyes closed and continue breathing. Breathe in deeply through your nostrils all the way to the bottom of your lungs, and exhale slowly through your mouth. You will feel a sense of flow begin to happen within you. Your body is emanating energy. It is the life force within you. It is your electrical matrix which keeps all the cells together. Imagine the tingling is caused by the cells coming alive. Smell the energy as it emanates off you. Keep coming back to "sensing" the energy. It almost pulses off your body in waves. It's very subtle. Tune into this. Register what it feels like.

Addendum

Find yourself going deeper into yourself. Sense the energy coming off your body. Conscious awareness is being consciously aware of what is going on around you and within you. Sense the pulses of energy coming from you. If you perceive something, slightly open your eyes, or keep them closed if you can, and write the perception on your pad of paper. Keep going deeper within yourself. Continue with the breathing; notice if it has changed. Perhaps you notice the slowness of it and the lack of breathing. It is the breath of God nourishing you.

Now, with your eyes still closed, starting with your feet, slowly scan your body. Use your internal senses. You will discover areas of discomfort or areas that need work. Slowly work your way up, exploring your body in its entirety. Say to it; "Talk to me. Tell me or show me what you want to show me or tell me." Keep going back to your body. If you perceive something, write it down. As you scan your body, repeat, "Talk to me. Tell me or show me what you want to show me or tell me." In your mind, listen to the silence, and pay attention to the pictures, sounds and colors that come forth.

Focus on this scanning process while working your way up your body, looking for information, as you say, "Talk to me. Tell me or show me what you want to show me or tell me." Practice quickening this process by moving your awareness faster. Stop at any spot you feel dysfunction. Keep talking to It to gain insight. You will perceive answers. When you have worked your way all the way up, slowly open your eyes. Slowly open your eyes.

Read what you have written. Does it make sense to you? Does it provide you with a different understanding?

II. Divine Self (Egg Exercise)

To begin, turn down the lights. If you do not have a tape, please ask a partner to begin reading the exercise below:

Put your feet on the ground and your hands on your legs, either up, or down, or clasped or fingers touching, whatever is comfortable. Just breathe in through your nose very slowly and slowly out of your mouth. Close your eyes. Breathe in and out slowly.

In ancient writings, the egg represents the one who has attained self-realization. The egg has always been the symbol of truth. This exercise is designed to bring you to a conscious atonement, or at-one-ment, at one with health, clarity of mind, deep visualization, peace, and awareness to see the light within. To the initial experience of contact with Self or the conscious divinity within. To the Nameless One, as mystics of old called It and its embryonic state that composes the universe. To the fluidity that carries the mind of the Nameless One that we dwell within. You will experience an overall sense of well being and peacefulness within. You may also see things, and experience changes in your mental perceptions within two weeks of practice. You may notice a slight glow in a darkened room, a light around yourself during or after the exercise while in a darkened room. This is a natural result of practicing this exercise.

Addendum

This is a true spiritual exercise in a mystical form for a greater effect. You may experience improvement in health, and well being as a result of this exercise. These spiritual exercises are your opportunity to attain self- improvement, and should not be taken lightly. The more you practice, the more you will be transformed. It will quicken your mental and spiritual growth and even your reality. Your spiritual senses will not be externalized, rather internalized through heightened awareness of the Divinity Within. Conscious application of this exercise for twenty minutes a day will enhance your awareness within of the Divinity Within, or what is known as Self or The Nameless One. Use moderation in the practice of this exercise. It should not be done more than twice a day, or for more than five days in one week. As it is written: Nothing Secret will remain hidden. It is through Self that all things will be shown.

Let us begin. Sit in a relaxed position, in a straight-backed chair, feet flat on the ground. Let your arms drop and then your hands. Let's clear your mind now. First breathe in slowly and gently in through your nose and out through your mouth. It is written that God, the Nameless One, breathed through the nostrils of man and woman and gave them life. If this is true, then we are breathing in the breath of God. Breathe in slowly through your nose, and gently out through your mouth. Breathe deeply down to the lower abdomen. With each exhalation, feel all tension leaving and your body becoming more relaxed with each breath. You will find yourself becoming lighter and more euphoric.

You might feel the sensation of a slight electrical charge silently flowing through the terminals of your fingers and your toes and right below the surface of your scalp. The feelings are the fluid of the spirit moving through you. There is no need to consciously let it flow out of you. Feel it well up within you. Continue with a very slow breathing pattern throughout the exercise.

Imagine a slow series of waves moving through your head. Become comfortable with it, let it flow freely. This will allow your cellular consciousness to shift without interference. Now be aware of the waves as they slowly move downward into your throat and through your spine. Downward through your chest. Down through your arms and hands from your chest to your lower abdomen. Let it sit there and feel the waves from your lower abdomen to your ligaments and muscles that bind your hips as it surges through your legs and down to your feet. Allowing the fluid of the spirit to well up from within, imagine these waves going through your entire body, from head to toe. Your whole body is becoming more relaxed and lighter and clearer. Stay conscious of your breathing. Feel the clarity and lightness in your entire body. Visualize yourself within an oval-shaped egg filled with clean, clear effervescent, bubbly light. Subtle light is emanating from around you. This light creates a shell around you, a shell composed entirely of light. You are actually seeing your true self with light emanating forth as you watch this experience. Now imagine yourself standing or sitting or even suspended there. The experience will be unique unto yourself. Continue to breathe slowly in through your nostrils the breath of God, the breath of the Nameless One, of the Universe and slowly out through your mouth through which the Word comes forth. Slowly become one with the light of the shell around you. Watch the light from within pulsate outwards. Focus on the pulsation. Watch particles of light illuminate in the way that a match flares into brightness. The tiny particles of light, in that moment, create a series of waves. You become enlightened within the form you carry. Watch your arms reach up into it. Feel the sensations of the light carry through your being of clear form. Feel it flowing freely. Now, step out. Move out of the shell. Be aware of the light from your form. Feel the emanations from within you coming through you. Feel the joy of its expression around you. Very slowly move in and out of the shell. This will help you adapt to it and it to you; the shell, too, has a living consciousness. Experience the freedom and joy and health of what you truly are, what you see inside and outside the shell. Experience the peace, quietude, intelligence, wisdom and consciousness of the subtle light and its life that gives you life. Now go back into the shell. Slowly bring this consciousness into your physical being. Remember your experience from within. Feel it, sense it, and let it live still within you. As you do, you bring this consciousness back with you into the atmosphere that emanates around you. Slowly come back. As you do, bring this consciousness with you. Slowly come back. Slowly open up your eyes. Sit still for a few moments.

Addendum

Take a little time to recoup. Stand up slowly and move around. When you are feeling ready, you may continue to the next exercise.

III. Flow of Life

A contemplative imagery exercise

Part 1

Begin to quiet down inside.
Let your eyelids drop and relax.
Breathe slowly and evenly...
In through your nose and out through your mouth.
Slowly and evenly...
Begin to feel the flow of life through out your
Body...
As it begins to flow...
You begin to get in touch with it... the flow.

From your heart, know that
You can feel a sense of love...
The Love that God might possibly have for you,
We know that this love is hidden within the
Deepest recesses of our heart...

Let the love slowly come out from your heart into
The surrounding areas in your chest,
And it begins to spread outward,

Know that in our natural spiritual state, we too are
Composed of effervescent light filled with Its joy of
Being,
Naturally fulfilled within the love of God,
And that initially we came forth from that love.

Addendum

This life, comes from within the mind of God,
Of pure life and consciousness, from the mind of
God

The clear feeling, the euphoric feeling that we are
Sensing, Is a result of opening your heart and
Mind to it
Trusting it, allowing it,
And allowing your true Self to
Be fulfilled with the love of God within.
And it filling and being fulfilled... Within You.
Get comfortable with your Self, and let your Self
Become a friend to you, watch yourself becoming
More quiet.
Allow It to love you.
Let the flow of God's love express Its Self in you...
Naturally and without your interference.
Breathing slowly and gently
That this flow might move freely in you.
In Its expression of love in you.

Allow all the thoughts... of other things,
Other times and other places to just flow away
And watch them dissipate into nothingness,
That you may begin to focus... on your true Self.

The feeling and the senses within it...
Sense the fear of doing this exercise, of letting go of
Everything else.
Watch the fear melt.

Allow your body to relax, feeling your muscles and
Feet and arms and hands as they keep dropping,
Let them drop even more so.

As you watch the tensions and worries of the day...
Of life.
Watching them flow slowly away...from your
Awarenesses and your body.
Feeling the flow of life flow through you as the
Trust of the fear lessens within you, and the
Godliness within you becomes more manifest.

Part 2

Begin to feel the slight electrical charge as it feels
Prickly
In your hands and in your feet and below your
Scalp.

Focus on your hips
And focus in the pelvic area of bones and muscles
And small organs within.

Visualize a nerve network almost like roots
Growing through the muscles, the bones of your
Thighs and your legs, as they develop and search
For their source of life... Just as roots do for water,
Flowing and searching and reaching down into the
Earth
As a conscious network of veins and capillaries...
Sending the roots down through your body and
Spreading down into the raw fertile earth
As they branch out in search of life...
Through the earth, and growing deeper...
The roots of a mighty tree.
Imagine your roots going down through the many
Layers of the earth.

Addendum

Down through the layers of the soil, through the
Sand, the silt, the gravel and the stone...
Reaching deep into the earth towards its core.

Know that the entire earth contains magnetic
Energies and that these energies are also naturally
A part of you.
Begin to feel the magnetic energies of your body
As they are also a part of you... to draw upon
Freely.
Know also, that the consciousness of the earth
Energies are magnetically attracted to you too.
And that your body feels and knows that too.

Feel your roots growing downward,
Moving through the depths of the earth until they
Begin to enter the periphery of a mass...
As though the mass carries a massive presence
Of fire and magnetism.

As your roots just begin to break thru the periphery
Of the mass,
These roots also begin to connect with this mass of
Energy within the earth
You begin to sense and see... that it is a deep shade
Of blood-red and gold energy. And it carries the
Sound of soft and powerful rumblings.

Addendum

Try to perceive this energy mass vibrating eight
Times in a second
And as it vibrates, it helps us to keep our own
Body's cycle near a rate of sixteen pulses in a
Minute.
Watch it and feel it as it feeds your pulse of life.

This mass vibrates at the same frequency as a
Naturally healthy body.
And as your roots enmesh into the mass of energy
And become one with the mass,
They automatically attune to the vibrational
Pattern of this the mass of energy.

This mass is the earth's blood, the flow that
Sustains all life on earth.

Pull this blood red and gold of the earth up into and
Through your roots and nerves.
Watching the energy as it moves up through this
Network,

Slowly at first,
Begin to feel the sensation of the bottoms of your
Feet wanting to open wider... as though they have
Vents...
Thirsting for this life.

As you begin to trust it,
Feel it freely flowing more into your feet,
The more your vents open the less fearful it will be.
Imagine yourself wanting more of it

Addendum

Feel the magnetic blood-red and gold flowing into
Your ankles, up to your legs, up through your
Thighs and into the muscles that bind your hips.

Feel it flowing into your belly, and slowly into your
Solar plexus area, and then permeating into your
Chest cavity,
Flowing slowly... into your heart.

From your heart through your arms and from your
Arms as they fill,
Permeating this life flow into your shoulders and
Up into your throat and then into your spine from
Top to the bottom and back up again into your head
As the mass slowly swirls within you, as it gives
You life.

Feel your heart fill with this blood-red and gold
Energy of the earth.

Notice the feelings that this magnetic energy
Creates in your body... as it brings you to greater
Realities and sensations,
A different understanding.

Notice the sensations,
You may be feeling a gravitational pull to this
Source of life from the earth.

Allow this earth energy to gently warm the inside
Of your chest and heart as you begin to feel it...
Feel this energy, as it gently and pleasantly warms
Your chest.

As it flows throughout your body and heart, in
Warmth.
As you feel your heart pumping in strength of the
Flow.
Feel the warmth of the flow of the energy moving
Through you.

Part 3

Turn your attention to the top of your head.
Picture a slightly glazed window in the top of your
Head...
And look through the window outward.
Try to decipher what you are seeing as you look
Outward.

Watch as the window's glaze... dissipates, to
Clarity.
And that there is no longer the obstruction,

Feel the flow of light,
Its waves and its particles of energy...
Beginning to flow through you.
Envision this light as effervescent clear glistening
Light,

And in Its wisdom,
It will help you to become more aware of the
Manifestation of the Godliness within you.

Addendum

Slowly bringing the flow of the clean clear
Effervescent light...
Into the top your head, and slowly down through
Your spine.
Imagining your spine as it is filled with this clear
Healing light.

The more you allow it to manifest within you,
And permeate you, exhilarate you,
Notice how differently you feel.

Experience this healing light filling your entire
Being
As it begins to freely flow throughout your body,
Without resistance.
As its healing light generates into your entire
Being,
Also watch as it generates outward from your
Body...
And around you into your energy fields which you
Generate.

Continue to bring this light through the top of your
Head,
Down through your spine.

Notice that your heart is also full of light
Sense how it feels as it fills and nourishes your
Heart.
Let the sensations expand,

Allow it to completely fill your chest cavity,
Saturating you... with clear effervescent light.

Part 4

Once again, from your feet, pull in the deep blood-
Red and gold earth energy and its magnetism...
Up through your feet,
Up through your legs and up into your pelvic area,

Moving towards the stomach and into the chest...
Bringing it more into your heart and saturating it.

Try to visualize and imagine the mixing of both
These energies,

Of the clean clear, effervescent healing light
And the deep blood-red and gold earth energy...
Both swirling within the heart, blending together.
As the swirling mixture within your chest
Fills your heart.

Watch as the valves of your heart open fully,
Distributing the mixture of magnetism and light.

As it is carried into the vessels, the veins and the
Capillaries... into the cells of your body.
Throughout the wholeness of your body.

Sending this blend of energy down through your
Arms and legs
As it flows to the very tips of your fingers and toes.
And you feel your fingers and toes and scalp with a
Slight electrical sensation.

Part 5

Now, silently and slowly, bring your hands together
Barely touching...
And gently rub your hands... barely touching palm
To palm.

As you keep your hands still, continue to visualize
The pulling through your feet the earth's
Magnetism
With the electrically charged energy of light flowing
Through you
As they mix together,

Breathing deeply and slowly,
In through your nose, down to the lowest part of
Your belly, slowly, out through your mouth.

Slightly and slowly pull your hands apart... only
Three to five inches at the most,
Feeling the energy surging ... filling your hands
And your wrists.
Feel the small mass of energy between your
Hands...
At the periphery of it, as you slightly move your
Hands... Slightly closer and slightly further apart –
It is not necessary to overdo it.

Feel the magnetic pull of energies between your
Hands,
As you bring your hands slightly closer,
The attraction.

Addendum

And feeling the repulsion of the pulse at the further
Distance
As you slightly separate them.

Very gently, feel this energy on the surface of your
Hands.
Feel how in some way, it might be affecting you.
Get to know it a little.
Try to understand it.
This is the life-force that you carry fully embodied
Within.

This energy is your gift, your very life.
When in times of sickness and distress…
It slightly deteriorates and needs to be re-supplied.

When it is totally depleted through the lack of
Creativity and oxygenation and blood flow in the
Body and brain, we cease to exist.

This energy is in every cell, between every cell,
It also forms your electrical matrix within and
Around your body
And extends outward into and thru the universe.

It is the energy field that is able to carry the
Information of your life into the aura,
The information of the morphic field within and
Around you.

Take a moment to perceive it.

Addendum

Now, gently place your hands on your lap.
Focus again on pulling up the deep red and gold
Energies of the earth.
From that mass of energy deep within the earth,
Into your body and again filling your heart
Focus again on the luminous electrically charged
Light flowing into your head...
And also flowing into your heart.
As you watch the swirling motion inside your heart,
Warming, opening and melting the layers of veils
That have been created to hide the love of God
Within,

Of what you thought and have been taught was
Protecting your Self from the world of hurt.

Feel the love of the radiant sun,
In all Its magnificence,
And Its manifestation of the Godliness,
The divinity within, bringing life into your heart,

Feel it fill your heart,
And your body,
And the many fields that emanate forth from you
Around you. Try to imagine how it might feel to
You...living within the mind of God
The unlimited magnitude of the information that
Might be offered to you.

Addendum

Part 6

Experience the gentleness, the joy, the reality of
This world...
Knowing now that we have a choice of which world
We choose to live within.
Take a moment to enjoy this.
Try to feel it with all your heart. Open your heart.
This is your living God,
Unconditionally loving you and giving to you,

In the way that you always have wanted to feel...
And to know Its love

Feel Its love within you,
Expressing Its love to you.
And when you get ready to come back to the room,
Slowly open your eyes...
And bring this love back with you...
Slowly open your eyes.
And bring Its love back with you...

Begin to come back now.
When you are ready, slowly come back to this room
And slowly open your eyes.

Addendum II

Quick Reference Guide to *Creator*
Exercises

Addendum

Addendum

I. Your first exercise: Focus on yourself

Here is an exercise that may be difficult to practice at first, but will have definite long-term benefits in your life:

> Choose the habit that you dislike most about yourself. Keep going back so you can remember when it started, its initial process, when you first began applying that habit in your life. Then ask yourself, "Why did it start?" Wait until you remember, which means to bring the members back together. By seeing, hearing, feeling or knowing, the dynamic sense that is most strongly recognized within you will reveal your answer. You can then get an understanding of how this particular habit has affected you in different aspects of your life.
>
> You will find yourself reflecting on the current manifestation in your thinking. When this happens, take that which you have just perceived and literally watch the situation unfold objectively. Review that dynamic remembrance as if it were the first time that you were experiencing it. See if you can find the actual causal moment in your life that led to you to carry the habit with you throughout life, that contributed to who you are and why you are what you are today. If indeed you have found the causal moment, watch what happens in your life with the revelation as it is "to be revealed within." In that moment a healing has actually just taken place. It has been intended to change your life for the rest of your life!

Addendum

This process is so simple and unique, and your transformation has only just begun. The transformation changes your mental perceptions and your emotional reactions to them. Your thinking processes may have produced biological effects within your body that manifest in the destruction of the physical being; the destruction you may have already experienced without knowing, which ultimately leads to the body's death. This exercise builds your ability to watch and perceive sundry ways to go through your individualized metamorphosis.

The idea is to watch the process objectively, without becoming involved in the dramas and traumas you witness. This is not possible unless we try this as a simple exercise and realize that in reality, there is nothing to fear. The truth does not kill or mentally harm us, nor can it make us sick, we do this to ourselves. The truth helps you to see yourself and thereby sets you free.

II. Conscious Awareness
   (Exercise 1)

Please read this in its entirely before you begin.

Stand facing a partner. In order to develop your intuitive awareness and meditative skills, we must first discuss conscious awareness. Conscious Awareness is the state of being consciously aware of what is going on around you and within you either in the conversation or actions in and around you.

Look your partner in the eyes and keep watching them. You must be able to control and stop yourself and become aware of what is happening within you, with you and around you. I want you to consciously stop yourself in the conversation you are now having when another person is in front of you.

Look deep into his or her eyes. Stop your thinking process that is wrapped up in the conversation. Stop the thought process and go within yourself and see what is really being said and what is really being done within you. Watch the other person think. Try that for just a moment. That is all that is needed, a moment in your life.

Go within yourself. You will see that moment has no specific time or duration. Watch you partner within. Surrender to your Self for this insight. Communicate with it within your mind and as you do, feel the warmth and the flow of it flowing freely through you. Unbeknownst to you, you will then be taken into this process and you'll be able to tune into a new, more real conscious awareness.

Addendum

With all your heart and soul, feel the love coming forth from within you. Consciously talk to It from inside your head. Express to It within yourself your need to love and listen as It tells you Its need to love you. Realize It as a close friend. Become aware of it. You can almost touch it. This is what awareness is. You are taking it on, you are clothing yourself with it. That's awareness. Let it flow through you. Let it live through you. Let it love you. Feel the love of it. Let it finally express to you Its love for you that you have never felt before. Now, come on back.

Addendum

III. Retrospective Exercise

What helped me learn to have concentrated focus was this "Retrospective" exercise. This exercise is to be done when you lay down to go to sleep for the night. It will increase your ability to focus. Have your eyes closed or open, it doesn't matter. See yourself in what you are doing at that moment. Then go back through your day, remembering one fairly significant event that happened right before bedtime. Don't get wrapped up in it. Pretend you are watching a movie when you are recalling this event. Perhaps it was a conversation that occurred, or you participated in an action that led to a significant outcome. Now, go to the event that was significant or fairly significant that happened prior to the first one. Something that was upsetting, something you argued about, something you said or thought that was of either a positive or negative nature. Then remember something that happened prior to that, working your way all the way back to when you first awakened for that day.

At first you may not be able to put things in their exact order, but that doesn't really matter. You will find yourself achieving a more precise order as you practice this exercise day after day. It will take care of itself. This is a fantastic exercise. Your memory will be so amazing and your dynamics will bloom magnificently. You will have a knowing that will develop from this retrospection that will be an important part of you for the rest of your life.

At the end of the exercise, you are going to take everything you recognized in that retrospection and say, "O.K. God, here are all the good things and not-so-good things that happened in my day. Here's the great me and the not so great me. Take it all, gather it all together and

239

cleanse it for me. Wash it for me, scrub it, launder it and put it into its place so I can see how it turns out the next day."

Addendum

IV. Conscious Awareness
(Exercise 2)

As an example, try this exercise for one minute. Sit quietly and think of nothing. Now notice all the conversations you're having in your mind. I want you to consciously stop yourself from any of these conversations. Stop yourself from being wrapped up in your conversation. Just watch yourself. Stop the thinking process that is wrapped up in that conversation. Stop your thought process and see what is really being said and what is really being done. Next, watch yourself as another person talks. Try it for just one minute. Concentrate on what is really happening. This is all that is needed, one minute in your life. You will notice how busy and active things seem around you. You may think you have no control over what one says, or what one thinks. Think again. We can actually stop our thoughts in their tracks. We can decide whether we want to think (or say or do) that specific thought (or word or action.) We can change it any time we want, that is our free will. You will soon become aware that one minute does not, in actuality, have a specific time element or duration. Actually, there is no time in the non-linear world.

Addendum

V. Conscious Awareness
(Exercise 3)

Here is the exercise: Watch what is really being said and done around and within you. Now, think of your Self inside, not the "little" you but the "big" Self that resides inside. Totally surrender to Self. Constantly love it and let it know you love it. Feel its constant warmth and flow. Now watch and feel the scene of the conversation. Unbeknownst to you, you will be taken into this process of expanded awareness and you will be able to tune into a new, more real conscious awareness. With this experience, over time, your times of dramas and traumas will fade away. What was your experience? Reflect for a moment on your experience with this exercise.

The more often you practice this simple exercise, the greater effect it will have in your life which has previously been so full of reactions and disappointments. You will begin to experience a sense of relative indifference to those old dramas, the situations to which you previously reacted. Now, with your heart and soul, feel the love coming into you. It is your new clothing. Consciously talk to it from inside your head, there's no need to talk out loud, and realize that it is a close friend. In becoming aware, you will pick up more. You will realize more, you will know more. That is what awareness is. You are taking it on; you are clothing yourself in it.

Think of your Self inside. Love it constantly and let it know you love It. Feel the warmth and flow of it. It flows constantly. Now as you watch what is really happening within and around you, there is a shift.

Addendum

VI. Grounding Exercise

Here is an exercise that is good for you to practice to experience what the healing energy feels like to you. This exercise also happens to be helpful for those with moderate dyslexia and it's good for calming an emotionally chaotic state, or an over-stimulated state, what I sometimes refer to as a "bombarded mind." Here is a "grounding exercise."

The pads of our fingers act as terminals which transmit a current. They also are receivers for current. The first three fingers, the thumb, forefinger and the middle finger, carry the greatest current. You can "feel" through the fingertips. A lot of nerve endings are located here for that purpose. What I've done with this exercise in the past seems to help relieve others of their feelings of chaos and confusion. When I've taught this exercise in the past, it helps many people understand what energy and light feel like.

The left hand is a receiver. The right hand is a transmitter. Historically, you gesture hello with the right hand. You are sending or transmitting a blessing to that person. The right hand is the giving hand, the left hand receives. In this exercise, take your right hand and hold the first two fingers about one inch apart and gently place them about one to one and a half inches above the eyebrows. You'll notice there are two slight indentations on your forehead where they seem to naturally fit. You can do this anytime, anywhere. Barely touch your forehead with these fingers. If you leave your fingers there for a little while, you will begin to feel a slight sensation in your fingers and/or in your head that will build up and then disperse. You are dispersing chaotic energy. The effect you get depends on your needs at that moment. Sometimes it takes five seconds to complete, sometimes a little longer.

VII. Five-Finger Exercise

This is a simple exercise that allows us to feel the energy, the light, the presence of the Divinity Within. Again as you begin this exercise, your hands and fingers will be barely touching. There is no need to rub your hands together to gather an electrical charge. Simply place the five fingers from each hand together in a makeshift tent. You can have them up or down, but don't let your hands touch silk or wool because that will create an unnecessary discharge and diminish the effect of the exercise. Don't press your fingers together, barely hold them there. Then hold this position until you feel the full effect. You'll notice a feeling of heat or vibrational sensation between the palms even if you have cold hands. Notice how it begins to build. It will increase. The palms will begin to tingle a little bit and more life force will flow into the blood. Wait there until you feel the flow in your fingers or your hands. Actually, you are assisting the life force and its flow. Your hands can be up or down, whatever is comfortable for you.

VIII: Energy Stabilizing Exercise

To complete this exercise, you will need a partner. Stand up facing one another.

Take hold of the other person's hand. Cross your arms so you are holding your right hand with their left hand, and your left with their right hand. Relax and close your eyes. Breathe in very slowly. Breathe in through your nose all the way down to your belly and gently and slowly out through your mouth. No heavy breathing. No hyperventilating. Slow and easy. Feel a lightness filling in your head. I want you to become aware of your partner's size, their shape and their temperature. Try to tune into that world, just for a moment. Now begin to feel the energy flow between you as you are becoming more one with that person, less threatened by that person. Really get into it. Concentrate on the energy flow between each of you, become one with it. The less resistance, the less threat, the less fear, the greater the flow. Let it flow. There is nothing to be afraid of.

Try to get in touch with the energy pull of that flow, of that energy called gravity. And in that you will feel the weight of its magnetism. It's a flow that is being established. Let it come into you. Don't restrict it. Feel it flowing freely. Tap into that flow a little bit. Open the bottom of your feet as if they are vents and allow the earth's gravity to enter you. See it, imagine it, feel it as a flow melting through you, flowing up through you like lava. Into your muscles, your bones and nerves. The vents in your feet will open up wider and wider. Feel the weight of it, the raw power of it. Let it flow up through your ankles, your lower legs. It might feel uncomfortable at first, bear it out. It will break through finally. Your knees, going up into your thighs, your hips, settling in your belly or lower back. Now feel it flow up through your chest and upper back and shoulders. It's a flow. It's magnetic. Let it flow through your arms and elbows. There are little logjams it will break through. Let it flow through your forearms, your wrists, your fingers, your hands. Let it break through. Nothing can stop it. And finally into your partner's fingers. Now that the flow is started, notice your breathing. How slow it is, how soft it is. Slowly open up your eyes.

Addendum

IX. The Palm-to-Palm Exercise

Stand up and face your partner. Make sure you are in a quiet environment so you can focus more easily. Place your hands in the "Pat-A-Cake" position. Bend your elbows at a 90-degree angle and turn your hands so one of your palms is facing the ceiling, the other facing the floor. Put the left palm up and the right palm down. Have your partner do the same so that your palms face one another's. Your palms should not be touching. Hold your palms one inch to one and a half inches away from your partner. Do not make physical contact.

Close your eyes. Begin to feel the energy between your hands. Feel it on your palms. That's the energy that's within you that is waiting and begging for you to give. It is the life force that is flowing between you. That's the flow of energy. Slowly start to move up and down a little bit. Feel this on the skin of your hands. Move slowly. Continue to move your hands slowly up and down a little. Feel the attraction and the pull of the energy. It will feel like a pressure inside. You will feel something between your hands. Experience the inner and outer limits of the electrical matrix of body. Feel how great it is. How tall it is. Move your hands apart until you barely feel it and open your eyes to see how far apart your hands are.

You are feeling the electrical matrix we are all composed of and the extrusion of the spiritual body. Also, while you are doing this, if you feel something in a special place in your body, like your wrist, that is because you are un-log jamming something. The flow of energy is giving life, it is clearing the logjam which is in that spot.

The Art of Healing Products and Ordering Information

CREATOR
Paperback edition, 254 pages
Learn about the mind of disease. Discover how healing can be broken down into simple laws of application. Learn to apply healing for emotional and physical well being of your self and others. **$21.95**

THE DIVINE SELF
Audio cassette approx. 20 minutes
A guided meditation for revelation. It potentiates the growth of awareness of Self. Through this instructive meditation you can actually learn to experience the Divine Self within. **$12.95**

MUSIC of the SPHERES
Audio cassette approx. 20 minutes
The OM (AUM) has long been considered the mystical sound of creation. Music of the Spheres recreates the OM (AUM) in harmonious tones and waves that blend together to create a blissful state in the listener. **$12.95**

THE FLOW of LIFE
Audio cassette approx. 20 minutes
A Contemplative Imagery Exercise is an exercise designed to help the listener to achieve emotional, biological and physical health. Mystical in nature, it is designed to help the listener to achieve spiritual focus and spiritual well being. **$12.95**

HEALING in the NEW MILLENNIUM
Video (VHS) set of 2, total time: 2 hours and 12 minutes
A lecture given by Mark Earlix in Sedona, AZ. December 27th 1999. Esoteric dimensions that are of applicable use in the world of potential healing concerning perspective, emotional physiological and physical causal moments. **$49.95**

SHIPPING AND HANDLING:
ADD: $3.00 PER 1-3 CASSETTE TAPES
ADD: $3.50 PER VIDEO (VHS) SET
ADD: $3.50 PER COPY OF CREATOR

Science Of MAN (SOM): For information write to P.O. Box 206, Boring, Oregon 97009

The Art of Healing Inc. TM 1928 E. Highland, Suite 104-Box 144, Phoenix, AZ. 85016